Connecticut's

Seaside Ghosts

Donald Carter

4880 Lower Valley Road Atglen, Pennsylvania 19310

Schiffer Books are available at special discounts for bulk purchases for sales promotions or premiums. Special editions, including personalized covers, corporate imprints, and excerpts can be created in large quantities for special needs. For more information contact the publisher:

Published by Schiffer Publishing Ltd.
4880 Lower Valley Road
Atglen, PA 19310
Phone: (610) 593-1777; Fax: (610) 593-2002
E-mail: Info@schifferbooks.com

For the largest selection of fine reference books on this and related subjects,
please visit our web site at
www.schifferbooks.com
We are always looking for people to write books on new and related subjects.
If you have an idea for a book please contact us at the above address.

This book may be purchased from the publisher.
Include $3.95 for shipping.
Please try your bookstore first.
You may write for a free catalog.

In Europe, Schiffer books are distributed by
Bushwood Books
6 Marksbury Ave.
Kew Gardens
Surrey TW9 4JF England
Phone: 44 (0) 20 8392-8585; Fax: 44 (0) 20 8392-9876
E-mail: info@bushwoodbooks.co.uk
Website: www.bushwoodbooks.co.uk
Free postage in the U.K., Europe; air mail at cost.

Designed by Stephanie Daugherty
Type set in Burton's Nightmare 2000/NewBskvll BT

ISBN: 978-0-7643-3000-1

Printed in China

Acknowledgements

My heartfelt gratitude goes out to the wonderful members of the New England Paranormal Video Research Group; our Founder and fellow Lead Investigator, Matt Sinsigalli, our Sensitive Gail Syring, Public Relations and Media Director Cynthia Frawley, Video Technician Seth Kaplan, Audio Technician Haydon Hall, Investigators Tricia Briley and Trisha Vargas, and Energy Sensitive Jennifer Untied. I also owe a giant thank you to Kirsten Moorhead for her beautiful cover art. I could never have done this without all of you!

A very big *Thank You* is also due the kind folks at the Milford Historical Society for aiding my research and affording our team the opportunity of investigating their lovely colonial properties, the Stratford Historical Society for their helpful information and photo of the old Phelps Mansion, and of course my friends and family who never stopped believing. Last, but not least, I would like to thank my editor, Dinah Roseberry, whose kind advice and guidance helped make this book print worthy.

Contents

Introduction

" So, do you believe in ghosts?"
This is perhaps the most common question asked of me when someone finds out about my hobby of researching historical hauntings for a paranormal investigative team. I tell them that I'm an open-minded skeptic, which generally gets me a confused look. I must, therefore, explain further.

You see, I tell them, I believe in a soul. I also believe in the *possibility* of displaced souls; those beings whose energy (electromagnetic, spiritual, divine or whatever), through unfortunate circumstance, trauma, tragedy, unfulfilled purpose, or simply choice, have lingered in the land of the living after their mortal shells are lain to rest. Have I ever seen an apparition? No, I have not. Thus, I have not yet been converted to the ranks of the Believers.

NEPVRG Lead Investigators Matt Sinsigalli (far left) and author Don Carter (far right), during a televised interview with twin demonologists Keith and Carl Johnson of TAPS (middle).

Is it a quest for the truth, then, that motivates people like me? In part yes, but mostly I just enjoy a really good ghost story!

I joined the New England Paranormal Video Research Group (NEPVRG) in the summer of 2006, with the sole intention of writing a book about my experiences. I was just finishing my second college degree, a Bachelor of Arts in Ancient and American History, when co-worker Matt Sinsigalli told me about his group.

"Ghost hunting?" I scoffed, from my self righteous bastion of historical facts and data. "Aren't they the folks who go around trying to get pictures of orbs, and screaming and running out of abandoned homes whenever a floorboard creaks?"

Then we got to talking about Dudleytown, Connecticut's most infamous ghost town and something I had done a fair bit of reading on. When Matt asked what I knew about it, I smiled.

"You want the history or the legend?" I quipped. You see, I explained, they are two very different animals. The vast majority of the books on Dudleytown (and they are legion!) only print the legends and myths recycled from other writers, without referring to the primary documents. The deaths of the village's residents during its heyday, though all of natural causes, have since been embellished upon to reflect a more sinister light on this unfortunate little community. Some would have you believe that Gershon Hollister was murdered in 1793 (he wasn't, he fell off a ladder and broke his neck during a barn raising), that Mary Cheney committed suicide (she didn't, she died of a lung disease), and that General Swift's wife was standing on a porch in a Dudleytown home when she was struck by lightning (she wasn't... but then, you get the picture).

"So... it's all lies then?" he asked, naturally enough.

Well no, I had to admit. There were some strange occurrences at the place. Unfortunately, with a place like Dudleytown, fact and fiction become hopelessly interwoven in the majority of articles and books you'll read. Only one book on the subject, Gary Dudley's *The Legend of Dudleytown*, makes use of primary records and genealogical data in unraveling the myths. A History teacher from Texas, Dudley's interest in our little Connecticut "ghost town with the rep" was initially genealogical. While researching his own family tree, he began uncovering the truth about the Dudleytown residents, truth which had largely been ignored since the 1930s in favor of the far more sensational legends.

Unfortunately for poor Mr. Dudley and all his hard work, the legends were already being held as fact. There were sensational and wrong accounts told by many who had much larger marketing engines than he. So the scholarly work by Mr. Dudley was diminished.

The truly disheartening thing is that the public was misled— you see the Dudleytown story, the true and unadulterated story, is fascinating enough in its own right. Weird things did, in fact, happen. These things have just been embellished and enlarged upon by so many generations, that getting to the truth can now be painstaking. It's like unraveling the truth about King Arthur.

That conversation with Matt got me to thinking. There had to be a happy medium between good storytelling and responsible historical research, where it pertains to hauntings, curses and such. Like I said, I love a good ghost story as much as the next guy. But I also like to know what *really* happened.

And I think you will too. If you didn't, you wouldn't have picked up this book.

So I began researching places where witnesses had alleged ghost sightings, apparitions, and spectral voices. I dug into the printed histories, land records, newspaper archives, and genealogical records. I even began seeking out the really weird, twisted, and morbid stories from Connecticut's past and places where paranormal phenomena would be *likely* to happen.

I did all this for the NEPVRG. Meanwhile, I came along on some field investigations, to get the genuine firsthand experience of what paranormal investigators did. I learned to operate a digital camera, video camera, voice recorders, infrared technology, and a host of other gadgets. Matt and I met with members of Historical Societies, park rangers, security guards, restaurant owners, and private homeowners to gain permission to investigate sites we deemed worthy. We gave interviews to the media; television talk shows, newspaper journalists, and website hosts. I made a website. I even began interviewing new prospective members.

I found myself spending way more time and money on the hobby than I had ever intended. But you know what?

It was fun. Simple as that. Navigating an abandoned ghost town in the middle of the night after having read all about some horrible murder that occurred there a century ago... well, it thrilled some dark and secret part of me. It made me feel like an occult investigator in an H. P. Lovecraft story.

I was hooked.

So here I am, two years later, and you hold the results of my research and firsthand experiences in your hands. Some of the stories herein are of actual investigations I have been on with the NEPVRG. In those chapters, I have made every effort humanly possible to present the historical background of the site as truthfully and accurately as the available data allows. You will find copious endnotes here, referencing each of my sources. In other chapters, I have written about past supernatural events that lay in the annals of Connecticut's history and folklore. Though it is impossible to go back and recreate these events, I feel they make for an interesting narrative, and are genuine and cherished parts of the story of Connecticut.

I am hoping that historians and history buffs, folklorists, tourists, urban explorers, readers of the paranormal, and folk who just enjoy a good spooky story will all find something within worth reading. If you finish this book and I have successfully thrilled, enthralled, or merely amused you, then I am content. At least I kept you interested to the end.

Then, when you've finished, stand in front of a mirror and ask yourself: "Do I believe in ghosts?"

If your eyes shift upward, you're lying.

Chapter 1
Ghost Ship of New Haven

The New Haven colony had suffered severe economic hardships by 1646. Several investments had failed or depreciated, and the townsfolk had fallen on hard times. Several leading men of the town, with the blessing of the esteemed Reverend John Davenport, invested much of their wealth in one great gamble. The goal was to save the lagging economy of the young colony.

They built a freight ship of 150 tons in Rhode Island, with the intention of sailing her from New Haven's port to England with a majority of trade goods. These goods probably included a great many furs traded from the nearby Indians of Quinnipiac, much in demand in Europe at that time. Should the mission be successful, and the haul transported, the return investment would be a lucrative one indeed, reviving the lagging spirits of the New Haven colonists. Hopes and dreams of several hundred Puritan folk hinged upon their success.

A Captain Turner was enlisted to sail her, in company with prominent New Haven men; a Mr. Gregson, Mr. Lamberton, and five or six others. The need of the colony must have been desperate, for they could not wait for warmer waters or fair weather. The ship, therefore, embarked in the cold of winter, in January of 1647. Town folk were forced to chop ice in the harbor to free the ship from its moorings. Lamberton, who was master of the enterprise, doubted the seaworthiness of the vessel, and was heard to mutter, "she will prove our grave…"

New Haven's greatest minister, Reverend Davenport, lead the town in prayer saying, "Lord, if it be thy pleasure to bury these our friends in the bottom of the sea, they are thine; save them!" So, with hearts both fearful and hopeful, the New Haven Puritans bid the small crew a safe and prosperous voyage. All agreed that the most valuable cargo aboard were the menfolk, much respected and prominent in the town. They were hardy individuals of the sort that a fledgling community could not afford to lose.

The journey to England should have taken no more than three or four months. Everyone waited eagerly for word. Spring came and went with no word from England. Many began to fear the worst. More time passed, and still no word.

Fretfully, the New Haven folk began to pray, "that the Lord would, if it was his pleasure, let them hear what he had done with their dear friends, and prepare them with a suitable submission to his Holy Will…"

The following June, the little colony was shaken by a sudden thunderstorm, the like of which they had never seen. It came from the north west and raged so violently that many believed it would wipe the harbor town from the map. Lightning shot through the sky and thunder rumbled the very ground. And then, an hour before sunset, all was still. Folk emerged from their houses, timidly at first, to find that all was serene beneath a magnificent dusky sky… and in this sky, some spied a sight so amazing that they gasped aloud. Curiously, the rest lifted their eyes to see.

A ship sailed among the clouds, her shape and dimensions seemingly familiar. Her sails filled with a supernatural wind, as if from a great gale. She held a steady northerly course, while the stunned spectators watched for over half an hour. The ship then began to struggle as if in some unearthly storm. Her main mast suddenly snapped, then her mizzen mast fell and was blown away. Then the proud ship toppled and crashed into a dark cloud, her keel splintering. Stunned, the colonists below watched her doom. Gradually, the clouds dissipated leaving only a night sky.

But many among the spectators had recognized the ship's rigging and colors, causing them to exclaim, "this was the mold of our ship, and this was her tragic end!"

To this, Reverend Davenport solemnly declared, "God has condescended, for the quieting of our afflicted spirits, this extraordinary account of his sovereign disposal of those for whom so many fervent prayers were made continually."

Legend holds that the fateful ghost ship has been seen several times since then, throughout the centuries, playing out its tragic doom upon twilight skies above New Haven harbor. Look especially among the clouds, after a violent storm, in the dark gloom of a June sky.[1]

Chapter 2
For Whom the Bell Tolls

Want to see a real nineteenth Century steamship like the *Atlantic*? Take a cruise on the *Sabino* at Mystic Seaport.

It was Connecticut's worst disaster at the time and it spawned one of our state's most interesting ghost ship legends. The wreck of the steamship *Atlantic* upon the coast of Fisher's Island in 1846 cost the lives of more than fifty passengers and crewmen, including at least five women. Many of the dead would never be properly identified, too horribly mutilated in the disaster, their bodies unrecognizable to loved ones. Some believe the enormous bell that had been mounted on her deck still rings its distress call today and can be heard on stormy nights upon Long Island Sound.

Bound for New York, the *Atlantic* departed Allyn's Point at midnight, Wednesday, November 25. Captain Isaac Kip Dustan, an experienced and popular seaman commanded the vessel. The steamer stopped briefly in New London before attempting the Sound, at which point the weather began getting rough. At least two passengers decided to disembark at that time, rather than risk the gathering storm. Captain Dustan, however, was confident. Besides, he had a wife and children waiting for him at his home on Staten Island and he was anxious to rejoin them.

Things began to go wrong almost immediately.

Not more than ten minutes out from New London harbor, waves began buffeting the gallant steamship. One particularly strong wave rocked the ship dangerously and a loud crack was heard by many. Then, around 1:00 am, a hideous explosion rocked the ship. The steam box, or steam pipe (the cause has never been adequately determined) had exploded, causing many small fires upon the *Atlantic's* decks and leaving her without power at the mercy of the tempestuous sea. The captain was heard to exclaim, "She's burst her boiler!"

No passengers slept that night, the darkness rent by flashes of lightning and dangerous fires aboard ship. Scalding steam bursts erupted in passengers' cabins, causing injury and panic. By dawn's feeble light on Thursday morning, the last of the small fires aboard were discovered and extinguished by crew, all flaming portions thrown overboard.

Captain Dustan advised everyone, "Keep cool, gentlemen; you may depend upon our doing everything for your safety, and that we shall be the last to leave the boat—keep cool."[1]

But the worst was yet to come.

The storm still raged, indeed it appeared to be growing stronger. Two ships, the *Massachusetts* and the *Mohegan*, passed close enough to see that the *Atlantic* was in severe distress. Both, however, were unable to navigate the choppy waters close enough to be of aid to the *Atlantic's* passengers. When the *Mohegan* seemed about to make the attempt, Captain Dustan ordered the distress signal withdrawn, so as not to endanger a second vessel to the same doom. Captain Dustan ordered life preservers inflated and distributed among the many passengers and crew. He also suggested everyone grab a door or board large enough to stay afloat upon, in the event of shipwreck. When Reverend Armstrong, a clergyman aboard, called for a prayer meeting in the morning hours, he did so with the captain's blessing. All attended.

Reverend Armstrong, in his sermon reassured the throng with quoted Scripture and was heard to pray humbly, "Father, if it be possible, let this cup pass from me."

All day and well into the evening, the steamship was tossed, with the storm showing no sign of abatement. By 5:00 pm, the situation had worsened so that the captain ordered all freight tossed overboard and instructed passengers and crew to cling to whatever they could. The rocky shores of Fisher's Island loomed, as the *Atlantic* continued upon its inevitable, doomed course.

Despite the dropping of anchors, the storm-whipped winds and water dragged the steamer back and forth, closer and closer to the ominous breakers of Fisher's Island. Throughout Thursday evening and the early morning hours of Friday 27 November, terrified passengers awaited the coming collision.

Then, around 4:00 am, it happened.

Three times, enormous waves slammed the vessel into the breakers on the eastern side of Fisher's Island. The *Atlantic* struck, stern foremost, her anchor ropes snapping apart. Passengers screamed, dove for the illusionary shelter of splintering decks, or leapt into the Sound to try a desperate swim for shore. The enormous distress bell clanged its discordant gonging dirge for the doomed. Lifeboats were useless.

A mighty wave, like the hand of an angry god, lifted the steamship and smashed it apart on the rocks. She shattered in halves between the Ladies Saloon and the Clerk's Office. The ceiling of the Ladies Saloon collapsed immediately, instantly killing most of the women aboard, who had taken shelter within. Many passengers and crew were crushed to death in that eyeblink of time when the impact occurred, most were torn apart into unrecognizable pieces. One man, at least, was literally severed in half.

Of those not killed in the collision itself, many more found a cold watery death in the Sound, drowning as they attempted to swim to safety. Like the mythical Charybdis, the Sound greedily drank the lives of dozens of luckless passengers.

Captain Dustan was heard by one of his crew to call for a rope. When the man replied, "If I go for the rope we shall both be lost!" the captain yelled back, "Well then, save yourself!"[2]

Some lucky swimmers actually made it to shore. Half frozen, wet and shivering, they frantically searched inland for shelter. Residents of a nearby home found and rescued as many as they could, providing fire, blankets, and shelter.

After its mighty and futile struggle, the *Atlantic* sank beneath the waves and was no more. Or was it?

By daylight, the storm had abated enough to allow the *Mohegan* to seek out its lost counterpart. The crew of the *Mohegan* later recounted that they were able to locate the survivors not visibly, but *by the clanging of the* Atlantic's *enormous bell...*

Pieces of the steamship would later be found for miles along the beach of Fisher's Island. All but the heavy iron bell, sunk beneath the waves. By Friday afternoon, the *Mohegan* returned to New London harbor with the surviving passengers and crew, along with twenty-three dead bodies. Most of the bodies were too horribly mangled to identify. One, in fact, consisted only of a head, upper torso, and two arms, which was buried on Fisher's Island rather than transported. More trips followed, with many more bodies and cargo recovered. Among the dead were Captain Dustan and Reverend Armstrong, as well as all the women aboard. Estimated losses ranged from forty to fifty-five or more persons, with almost as many survivors.[3]

Captain Dustan's body was transported by the Long Island Boat to Greenport, then conveyed to his family at Staten Island.[4]

Mass funerals were held for the unidentified dead in New London, Norwich, and even as far away as Boston (where it is believed as many as thirty of the passengers may have come aboard). Particularly noteworthy are the sermons of two clergyman.

One, Reverend Kirk, was apparently a hellfire and brimstone preacher. His published sermon seemed to blame the disaster on the sinfulness of man; "God has sent many preachers, with soft voices, but they were not heeded, and he next speaks in the whirlwind and the tempest... He has more storms in his storehouse. Fire, hail and tempest all fulfill his will..." Of the greatly admired Reverend Armstrong, Reverend Kirk said, "God built a pulpit for him right by the gates of death. He preached there as a true soldier of the Cross. He believed and so he preached."

He concluded ominously, "... how indiscriminating is death. Many valuable lives perished there, and Providence is saying to us all, 'Be ye also ready!'"[5]

A sermon by Reverend Arms was far more somber, and lingered on the character of the much beloved captain, "I seem to see him still, walking the deck of the beautiful craft, which his own intelligent skill had planned. I see his noble bearing, his erect position, his commanding figure, his manly features, in which were blended intelligence and unaffected good will..."[6]

A month later, the brave steamer *Mohegan* was itself lost at sea. On Saturday 26 December, at around 3:30 pm, while running freight between New York and Bridgeport, it wrecked upon Gangway Rocks, not far from Sand's Point Light. Though conditions were clear and calm, a low tide caused the bottom of the steamer to stove in by way of submerged rocks. She ran aground at a place called Cow Bay, where she sank within two feet of her hurricane deck. Fortunately for the *Mohegan*, however, all persons aboard were safely rescued, with no serious injuries and no loss of life. Perhaps divine providence had watched over the *Mohegan's* little crew, who had striven so hard in the rescue of the doomed *Atlantic*, and had been saddled with the grisly task of transporting her horrifyingly mangled dead.[7]

A ghostly legend surrounding the *Atlantic* is still told along Connecticut's shore. None could account for the sound of the *Atlantic's* fog bell leading the crew of the *Mohegan* to the wreck site... a bell that had already been lost in the Sound. Some claim that the bell may have still been attached to part of the hulk, washed ashore and rolled by waves, so that it tolled loud and clear over and over again. Others are not so sure.

Indeed, fishermen, sailors, and others have claimed, in the century and a half since the wreck, to have heard the peal of the *Atlantic's* bell through the fog and waves, hauntingly morning her lost dead. The ghostly bell is referred to in a memorial to Captain Dustan, in New London. Inscribed in stone are the words;

> *"Far, far o'er the waves, like a funeral knell,*
> *Mournfully sounds the 'Atlantic's' bell.*
> *'Tis the knell of the dead, but the living may hear;*
> *'Tis a warning to all amid the opening year."*[8]

Race Rock Light

The *Atlantic's* story does not end there.

The area where the *Atlantic* went down, known as the Race, is a particularly hazardous one to mariners. Dozens, if not hundreds, of shipwrecks occurred upon the Race Rock reef. At least eight recently documented shipwrecks preceded that of the *Atlantic*, due to the fast moving current and the submerged stony reef. Yet the horrific loss of life from the *Atlantic* shipwreck, and the publicity it generated, finally convinced Congress to appropriate the necessary funds to build a lighthouse upon the deadly reef.

This lighthouse, known as Race Rock Light, marks the approximate spot where many of the *Atlantic's* passengers and crew met a watery death. It is said to be one of the most haunted lighthouses in the Sound, along with New London Ledge and Penfield Reef lighthouses.

The construction of Race Rock Light was not easy. The location caused many hazards for the workmen, and mishaps and minor disasters plagued construction for several years. At least two workmen lost their lives in the construction. By far, the foundation proved the most daunting part to build. Completion of the tower

Race Rock Lighthouse, built upon the same reef where the doomed Atlantic was destroyed and believed to be very haunted. *Courtesy of Dan Peeler*

and keeper's dwelling took only nine months, while construction of the foundation upon which they rested took seven years. Costs continued to rise with each new adversity, until the lighthouse was finally completed in 1878, more than thirty years after the *Atlantic* disaster, at a total cost of $278,716 (an extraordinary sum at that time!).

One of the last stone masonry lighthouses to be built, it gorgeously reflects the Gothic Revival architecture in vogue at the time. This style can clearly be seen in the pointed arches of the entry pavilion and lower tower, as well as the roof's carved rafter ends. Its granite walls present a grim, though elegant monolithic appearance, rising out of the sea with its flashing red and white light. The lantern rises sixty-seven feet above high water and can be seen for fourteen miles on clear nights.

Fog, however, appears to have been a consistent problem. The fog signal at Race Rock Light never worked quite right. Even after several repairs and replacement with a more powerful fog engine, it was still prone to malfunction without explanation. Often, the keeper had to resort to the auxiliary bell (established in 1896). This bell actually replaced the poorly running fog engine, which had been discontinued in 1897 until a new apparatus could be installed the following year. Even today, mariners report that the fog signal is nearly inaudible.[9]

This, of course, may explain the legend of the *Atlantic's* bell. When the fog siren failed, as it was prone to do, the tolling of a bell warned seamen of the deadly reef.

Even after the construction of Race Rock Light, the reef continued to claim lives. Lighthouse keeper Thomas A. Carroll, appointed keeper in 1880, drowned while trying to row back to the lighthouse from his Noank home during a storm in 1885. His body was discovered the following spring, washed ashore at Groton Long Point.

Most recently, The Atlantic Paranormal Society (TAPS) did an investigation of Race Rock Light for the Sci-Fi

Channel's popular reality show, *Ghost Hunters*. Their findings were startling, including a chair in the attic that appeared to move by some invisible force. This video is readily available online, for anyone who wishes to view it.

Race Rock Light certainly has a long reputation of being haunted. Some say the haunting is perpetrated by a victim, or victims, of the *Atlantic* disaster, others say that Keeper Carroll still remains, in spirit if not in body.

Chapter 3
Nightmare On Elm Street

The Phelps Mansion in its heyday, site of the "Stratford Rappings" haunting. *Courtesy of the Stratford Historical Society*

For several months in 1850, a preacher's home and family became the center of nationwide attention as "mysterious noises" and "unearthly doings" frightened and astounded the people of the sleepy little town of Stratford. Even a century and a half later, researchers can find no real explanation for the "Stratford Knockings" and other phenomena that plagued the home of Reverend Dr. Eliakim Phelps.

Some historians of paranormal phenomena have labeled the events at the Phelps Mansion typical of poltergeist manifestations, centering upon the reverend's eleven-year-old adopted son and sixteen-year-old adopted daughter. Others are not so certain, pointing out bizarre incidents which occurred at the mansion that may more properly be classified as a haunting by a mischievous spirit or demonic entity. Some folk have even suggested the perpetrator of the haunting to be none other than the ghost of Goody Bassett, a woman hanged for witchcraft in Stratford in 1651. Whatever the case, the Stratford happenings are certainly unique for their strangeness.[1]

The mansion formerly located at 1738 Elm Street, at what is now Rosemary Drive near Stratford's Shakespeare Festival Theatre, was built in 1826 for a Captain George R. Dowdell. While away on a sea voyage to China, his last before retiring, Captain Dowdell's wife outlined her unique plan for the home's construction. The hall was made seventy feet long and twelve feet wide, so that it would have the familiar length and feel of a ship's deck. The twin staircase was also crafted to simulate a ship's layout, so that the sea captain would feel as if he were walking to the hurricane deck on one side and the main deck on the other. A magnificent success, the mansion had Ionic columns fronting the exterior and was one of nineteenth century Stratford's most beautiful homes.

Reverend Dr. Eliakim Phelps, a retired Presbyterian minister, purchased the home in 1848. Born in Belchertown, Massachusetts, he had graduated from Union College in Andover in 1814 and was ordained at the First Church in Brookfield in 1816. He was installed over the Presbyterian Church in Geneva, New York in 1830 and received his Doctorate of Divinity in 1860, after which he transplanted to Plainfield, Connecticut. He served as pastor of the Huntington Church from 1847 to 1849, until his retirement at age fifty-nine.[2]

Widowed from a previous marriage, in which all his children had grown to adulthood and moved away (his son, Austin Phelps, became a Professor of Theology at Andover College), Reverend Phelps decided to remarry. He chose a bride much younger than himself who already had three children of her own; teenage Anna, adolescent Henry, and a girl toddler. They would also have a son of their own in 1847. Upon his retirement, Reverend Eliakim

Phelps moved with his young wife, adopted family, and infant son to Stratford.

Originally from the city of Philadelphia, the young wife did not adapt well to quiet, rural life in Stratford. She resented small town politics and grew bored with country life. Added to her frustration, her daughter, Anna, had an undiagnosed "nervous disposition." These factors, along with a mischievous adolescent son, were often given by skeptics as motivations for a hoax. The sincerity of Reverend Phelps seemed above suspicion by his contemporaries due to his good name and character, though many believed him the gullible dupe of his own family members. Whatever the case, events of 1850 at the Phelps Mansion soon had newspapermen and neighbors divided on the question of "haunting or hoax?"

The Reverend Phelps was also unusual for a Presbyterian minister in that he had a peculiar fascination with mysticism and the Spiritualist movement. He followed accounts of mediums, mystics, and spirit communications with avid interest. Some would later claim that this made him particularly susceptible to the machinations of young Anna and Henry, who would be blamed by several newspapers for the majority of unexplained phenomena that occurred. Believers in the Phelps Mansion haunting, on the other hand, see the Reverend's interest as a possible gateway for the mischievous spirits that soon plagued the family home.

In fact, only a week before the haunting began in earnest, in March of 1850, Reverend Phelps hosted a séance at his home. A visiting friend with similar interests in Spiritualism had convinced him to try spirit communication. The experiment had resulted in a few mysterious knockings, or rapping sounds, but nothing else of note. This amateur attempt at a séance would lead some to postulate that Eliakim Phelps unwittingly summoned the spirit himself.

Six days later, on Sunday 10 March, the haunting began. What followed, for the better part of a year, is a matter of debate to this day.

The Phelps family had just returned home from morning church services. Reverend Phelps was surprised to find that all the doors to the house, which he had carefully secured before departing, were unlocked and unbolted. Some of them were swung wide open and a strip of black crepe was draped over the knob of the front door. The minister initially suspected thieves or vandals. Cautiously, the family entered their enormous home only to discover that furniture had been overturned and flung about the house. They found also that dishes had been smashed, and books, paper, and clothing scattered about. Strangely, his gold watch, the family silver and loose cash had not been touched. This then, seemed to discount the possibility of thieves.

An even stranger revelation was discovered by Reverend Phelps when he investigated the upstairs rooms. A nightgown belonging to Mrs. Phelps had been stretched out upon a bed with stockings placed below and arms folded, as a human cadaver would be for burial.

After replacing much of the furniture and restoring the house as much as possible to its original orderliness, the family prepared to depart again for afternoon services. Reverend Phelps opted to stay behind and perhaps catch whatever mischief makers were responsible in the act. Mrs. Phelps and the children left for church.

Taking up a loaded pistol, Reverend Phelps hid in his study and waited. Hours passed with no sound or sign of movement within the house. Eventually leaving his study, Phelps was shocked to discover yet another mysterious bit of mischief.

In the dining room were what appeared to be several women, some kneeling and some standing. All appeared to be in a position of prayer, most holding bibles. Upon closer examination, he found that all were amazingly lifelike effigies fashioned from clothing belonging to family members and stuffed with various clothes, rags, and odds and ends. These inexplicable dummies had apparently been fashioned soundlessly while Phelps had waited in the nearby study, listening intently for any hint of movement.

For some reason, Reverend Phelps let the effigies remain in their postures. Over the next several weeks, many more of these effigies added to the growing total, always appearing when no one, apparently, was looking.[3]

These effigies alone separate the Phelps Mansion haunting from what many would consider to be "typical" poltergeist phenomenon. In almost every other way, whatever was responsible for the events of 1850 in the Phelps home seemed to follow the general guidelines, or "rules," of a poltergeist haunting. Invisible physical attacks upon the teenage daughter, Anna, and more violently upon her adolescent brother Henry, certainly fit the mold. Henry, especially, seems to have been the center of the phenomena, whether natural or supernatural, occurring in the home.

Almost daily, following the events of 10 March, objects appeared to be thrown or pushed by invisible hands throughout the house. Anna, at times, was pinched or slapped while lying in her own bed. Henry, who seems to have suffered most, was almost strangled in a pantry closet, where the family discovered him with a rope around his neck. Another time, Henry was stuffed head first into a water barrel and nearly drowned. Often, his clothing was shredded into strips upon his body, the strips then tied to whatever piece of furniture he may have been sitting on at the time. Once, while investigating journalists had visited the house, Henry went missing while flying a kite outdoors and was discovered buried in a pile of hay in the barn, in a semi-conscious state. On other occasions, he was reportedly seen by family members to be lifted up, levitated, or carried about the room by an invisible force.

Of course, many or all of these phenomena may have been the work of mischievous youth, particularly Anna and Henry working in concert to perpetuate the hoax. Some skeptical journalists were quick to point this out, as the situation gained more and more attention in the media of that time (namely, newspapers). Many credible and respected witnesses, however, were perfectly willing to put their names and reputations on the line to vouch for the authenticity of supernatural activity in the house.

It was not long before investigative and curious visitors from all walks of life began appearing at the Phelps Mansion. Reporters from the *Derby Journal* and the *New Haven Palladium*, were particularly outspoken in their separate beliefs on the matter. Learned clergymen from different denominations, professors, doctors, and other professional men of high standing came to the house, as well as mystics, mediums, and Spiritualists of every stripe. The only thing that all seemed to agree upon was the friendliness, sincerity, and apparent honesty of their host, Reverend Phelps. As to the integrity and veracity of Henry and Anna, well… that was a matter of debate.

Among the first to arrive at the home, at the request of Reverend Phelps, was another retired minister and personal friend of Eliakim Phelps, Reverend John Mitchell. Reverend Mitchell's initial theory was that trickery performed by the girl servant or the children was responsible. After the two ministers removed all likely perpetrators from the immediate area, the activity continued. After witnessing these flying objects firsthand, Reverend Mitchell became an ardent believer in the presence of one or more supernatural entities wreaking havoc in the house.

On 14 March, Mitchell and the Phelps family together witnessed forty-six objects seemingly drop out of the air and onto the floor of the parlor, an event presaged at breakfast when a potato plopped down from nowhere onto the dinner table. Many of the objects were apparently taken from other areas of the house and dropped from the air at random. Objects would continue to appear from apparent thin air through the days and weeks ahead, sometimes with strange hieroglyphs and indecipherable writing carved upon them.

While objects hurtled or drifted through the air of the house during the daytime, loud rappings or poundings sounded throughout the night. Many windows, pieces of furniture, and prized family heirlooms were destroyed in the process. Once, a fireplace poker was said to have hurled itself through a front window. Very little of this flying object phenomena was actually witnessed by reporters at the house, however. Most often, an object was heard to hit a wall or land upon a floor, only to be seen after the fact. This led many to believe that a human agent caused the object to begin its trajectory.

At some point, Austin Phelps, the grown son of Reverend Phelps from his first marriage and a Theology Professor from Andover, came to Stratford to investigate for himself. Like many others, he believed his father to be the victim of a hoax perpetrated by members of the minister's adopted family. He strongly disapproved of the negative publicity surrounding his aged and respected father and brought with him his uncle, Abner Phelps, a Boston medical doctor and legislator, to help debunk the whole affair.

Their first night in the home, they were awakened by a loud pounding from the front door. Upon investigation, however, they were unable to determine a cause. Indeed, even when one of them stood on one side of the door and one on the other, the pounding continued.

The following night, they heard rappings from upstairs and determined that the sound game from a banging on the inside of Anna's bedroom door. Instantly upon hearing a series of these rappings, they burst into the room, hoping to catch the teenager in the act. Anna, however, was in her bed, far from the door and under covers. The two men saw deep dents on the inside of the door, but could not determine an explanation.

Professor Austin Phelps and Doctor Abner Phelps left the mansion to return to Massachusetts, converted to the belief that the occurrences at the mansion had no explainable cause.

On Friday 15 March, the editor of the *Derby Journal*, H. B. Thayer, spent the night at the Phelps Mansion, with three other men, in an attempt to solve the "mystery." They, too, responded to Anna's room upon hearing rappings from within. They were also unable to determine the cause, and upon turning to leave the room had a brush and a comb thrown at them, apparently from some source other than the teenage girl. After exiting and shutting the door, the men heard a loud bang upon the door and rushed back in. Anna was in her bed, but flushed as if she had just been struck. Her cheek was perceived as being very red, and the noise discovered to have come from the impact of a large white pitcher against the door. The men decided that the pitcher had "been flung with a force which no delicate female could possibly possess," breaking off the handle and leaving an indentation in the clapboards a quarter of an inch deep. The men also determined that the angle of the trajectory which the pitcher must have traveled would have been impossible for anyone in the bed to have thrown.

The editor and his companions left the mansion the next day, mystified. The editors of the *New Haven Palladium, New Haven Journal,* and the *Courier,* unsatisfied with the *Derby Journal* editor's sensational account of what they assumed to be a hoax, decided to try their hand. They arrived at the Stratford home around 2:00 pm on Wednesday afternoon. They brought with them an Episcopalian minister.

It was during their visit that Henry went missing while flying his kite. They assisted in the search and found young Henry in the barn, in his semi-comatose state. During the time of their visit, Reverend Phelps recounted many of the instances of strange phenomena he had witnessed and showed them many of the damaged windows and objects about the house. The editors left after their brief stay without any definite conclusions and without having witnessed any extraordinary phenomena. Being much impressed with the courtesy and sincerity of Reverend Phelps, they hinted in their formal account of the visit that their respect for the reverend actually hindered any productive interrogation of his family; "We could not pursue our investigations as far as we desired, without seeming rude, or without abusing the courtesy extended to us, by appearing to suspect collusion among the members of the family."[4]

During the visit of the New Haven editors, the word "Selah" had been written on the stoop. Comparative analysis, as noted in the *New Haven Journal* editor's account of the affair, bore a suspicious resemblance to the handwriting of Henry, whom he supposed of being perpetrator of the hoax. The word Selah is Hebrew and is a very difficult one to translate. It can mean "stop and listen" or even "forever."

Even more interesting, the root of the word is "calah," which means "to hang." It is an interesting coincidence that young Henry was once found in the pantry with a rope around his neck, and Goody Bassett had been hanged for "divers witch-like arts" 200 years prior, less than a mile from where the Phelps Mansion then stood.

The *New Haven Journal* editor, however, was not impressed. He very blatantly stated, "From beginning to end, the history of this affair is a mournful commentary on human credulity and folly."

Reverend Phelps attempted another séance to communicate with the spirit. Though the entity allegedly showed signs of intelligence, its answers were often mischievous or nonsensical, often contradictory. A system of communication by which a numbered series of raps represented letters of the alphabet was established. Initially, whatever answered Phelps and his friends claimed to be a tormented spirit in Hell. At other times the spirit, when asked what it wanted, answered "a piece of pumpkin pie." Asked again, it answered, "a glass of gin." When asked why it disturbed the household, it replied, "for fun."

Sometimes, it seemed to write out its messages on paper, either through the medium of Reverend Phelps' own hands or through invisible means. Often these messages were indecipherable occult symbols or glyphs, other times they seemed to spell out brief messages in English. The Reverend quickly discredited these messages though, stating that: "I have become fully satisfied that no reliance whatever is to be placed on these communications..." and that, "it is the work of evil spirits." He went on to say, in a printed letter to the *New York Observer*, that "their communications are wholly worthless... often contradictory—often proven false—frequently trifling, and nonsensical..."[5]

Unfortunately, no written record survives of the actual messages, since Reverend Phelps meticulously destroyed all those that he found, believing them to be evil.

Worst of all were the attacks on the children. Anna was pinched, hit, slapped, and once, while sleeping, according to the editor of the *Bridgeport Standard*, had a pillow pressed down upon her face and tied around her neck with tape, an attack from which she nearly died. Attacks upon Henry were even worse, he was frequently strangled, struck, his clothing shredded, and nearly drowned.

The haunting appears to have been centered around the children. Indeed, it did not end until the family finally had enough and decided to move back to Philadelphia in October. Reverend Phelps remained behind while Mrs. Phelps left with the children, but whatever had created the mischief, be it human or otherwise, left with them. The minister saw no more supernatural occurrences or mysterious happenings while he remained alone, setting his affairs in order before joining his family.

The family returned briefly in the summer of 1851, but it appeared that the haunting was over. Reverend Phelps sold the house and took his family forever from Stratford, and Connecticut. Alfred E. Beach bought the house from Phelps in 1859. Several other owners occupied the mansion in succeeding generations, but no further outbreaks of rappings or poltergeist-style phenomena were reported. Eventually, the beautiful mansion was abandoned and fell into disrepair. It became the target of teenage vandals and thrill seekers. It was eventually demolished in March of 1972.[6]

Today, the spot where the Phelps Mansion once stood is

now Rosemary Drive. It is a private residential area, in which spiritographers and other interlopers are neither welcome, nor wanted. Nearby is Stratford's Shakespeare Festival Theatre.

According to several paranormal groups and personalities, the Shakespeare Theatre was itself the site of significant paranormal activity, and allegedly still is. The academy building, fronting Elm Street, bears a remarkable similarity to the old Phelps Mansion, though the four Greek columns of its façade are Doric, rather than Ionic. Unfortunately, the Theatre is now closed to the public and has fallen into disrepair itself. Pedestrians frequently stroll the quiet grounds of the academy and theatre proper, but the buildings themselves have been boarded and padlocked.

The location is also notable for another historic incident, the hanging of Goodwife Ruth Bassett (or just "Goody Bassett" to the locals) in 1651. The spot became known in Stratford's oral and written history as "Witches Rock," at what is now the intersection of Linden Avenue and West Broad Street, about three quarters of a mile from where the Phelps Mansion once stood. The rock itself was said to be a boulder that marked the spot, with indentations from Goody Bassett's fingernails from when she was dragged to the gallows.[7] The stone, however, was moved or destroyed during the construction of I-95 through Stratford in the 1950s.

Questions regarding the events of 1850 at the Phelps Mansion have never been adequately answered. Was the entire thing a hoax manufactured by Anna and Henry, perhaps to fulfill their mother's spoken or unspoken wish to leave quiet Stratford and return to the city? Was it a poltergeist summoned by Henry, or the psychokinetic energies of Henry or Anna? Was it a disgruntled spirit, perhaps one of the forgotten bodies buried along Elm Street during its colonial days (purportedly, much of Elm Street was originally used or this purpose)?

Or was it, as some claim, the vengeful spirit of Goody Bassett, returned from the grave 200 years after her execution for witchcraft, to torment and ruin the life of a Protestant minister, just as three such ministers had passed judgment upon her and destroyed her own life?[8]

Stratford's Shakespeare Festival Theatre, very near the spot where the Phelps Mansion once stood and also believed to be haunted. Note the similarities of its façade with the older photo of the Phelps Mansion.

Stratford's Shakespeare Festival Theatre, auditorium building. Grounds are open to the public, but the building itself is boarded, locked, and abandoned indefinitely.

Chapter 4
Midnight Mary

The infamous headstone of Mary E. Hart, known as "Midnight Mary" to locals in New Haven's Evergreen Cemetery. Stand upon her grave at midnight, legend says, and some horrible doom will befall you. Many believe she was buried alive.

It is doubtful if any single grave in Connecticut's seaside towns has generated as many legends as that of Mary E. Hart, located in New Haven's Evergreen Cemetery. She is better known to locals and Yale students as "Midnight Mary," around whose grave bizarre tall tales have grown for over a century. Many daring and foolhardy thrill seekers climb the iron fence of Evergreen Cemetery, to stand upon the grave at midnight and tempt the "curse" that supposedly befalls all who do so.

A basis for the curse legend can be directly attributed to the unusual inscription upon the large pink granite marker, which states, "THE PEOPLE SHALL BE TROUBLED AT MIDNIGHT AND PASS AWAY." Much has been made of this singular inscription, especially among those who see it as definitive evidence of a malediction. Persistent urban legends remain, growing in the retelling. The most consistently told, and believed, legend of all is that forty-seven year old Mary Hart had been buried alive! The buried alive story, combined with that of her ghost haunting the grave and a curse upon anyone who dares trespass have together generated a cycle of urban legends that continue today.

The quote itself is not some ancient curse or the last words of some poor soul convicted of witchcraft (of which Connecticut had more than its share!). It is an abridged Biblical passage from the book of Job, chapter 34, verse 20. The complete passage, in the King James original version, goes, "In a moment shall they die, and *the people shall be troubled at midnight, and pass away:* and the mighty shall be taken away without hand." The passage makes sense when one reads the rest of the marker.

> "AT HIGH NOON/ JUST FROM, AND ABOUT TO RENEW/ HER DAILY WORK, IN HER FULL STRENGTH OF/ BODY AND MIND/ MARY E. HART/ HAVING FALLEN PROSTRATE:/ REMAINED UNCONSCIOUS, UNTIL SHE DIED AT MIDNIGHT,/ OCTOBER 15, 1872/ BORN DECEMBER 16, 1824."

So reads her death inscription on one side of the large granite block, which she shares with one James P. Hart (died January 18, 1877 at age sixty) and his wife, Fidelia Pierpont (died August 12, 1885 at age eighty-five). A nearby headstone of the same style and same rosy granite is that of one Joanna Hart, presumably a relative, born in Berlin, Connecticut in 1782 and died at New Haven in 1870.

Mary's cause of death was a stroke, from which she eventually died at midnight. New Haven census records from 1850 through 1870 indicate that she twice lived with her brother James and sister-in-law (whose name in the censuses is given as Susan, not Fidelia, which may indicate that Susan was known familiarly by a middle name). Little is known of Mary's life until her death in 1872. She appears to have been a machine-stitcher and corset maker. This is all that historical research has thus far revealed about the life of Mary E. Hart, the rest is legend.

Supernatural legends surrounding Mary Hart's grave are legion. A little historical detective work can unravel some of these, revealing the grain of truth that spawned them. By far, the best account of these many legends is that compiled by David E. Philips.[1] The truth behind them can be found in researching available archives and documents, including articles in the *Hartford Courant*.

The first of these, that the family invented the enigmatic words on her tombstone about people being troubled at midnight and passing away, is already proven untrue. The words are part of the Bible passage already quoted. Unfortunately, many who have written of the "Midnight Mary" legends may be unaware of this fact.

The most consistent legend, of course, is that of live burial. According to the legend, Mary was not struck dead but had fallen into a state of suspended animation. Such incidents, though rare, are sometimes known to happen, and were extremely difficult for nineteenth-century doctors to diagnose or discover in time. Such an incident occurred in 1900, in East St. Louis, when Mrs. Christiana Hirth woke up from apparent death, just as the mortician was about to embalm her.[2] Other causes of a deathlike state, besides stroke, are lead poisoning and certain snakebites.

The tale goes on to say that Mary's aunt, on the night following the burial, had terrible nightmares in which Mary had awoken in her coffin and called desperately for help. The aunt successfully alarmed the family enough to order the grave exhumed. When the coffin was opened, they saw Mary's body horribly contorted, her fingernails broken and deep grooves clawed into the inside of the lid. To cover up their mistake, a death story was inscribed on her monument and the enigmatic message engraved above it as a warning.

Unfortunately, no evidence survives to support the live burial story, or exhumation, and the inscription can be easily explained by the hour of her death. The tale may very well be a Connecticut adaptation of a similar Maine legend, that of Mary Howe. Mary Howe was a spiritualist and medium who often went into trances, sometimes for a week or more at a time. In 1882, while in a deathlike trance, the local doctor of Damariscotta, Maine declared her dead over the protests of the family. She was buried, despite considerable resistance in the town from neighbors and friends, and the legend is widely known even today. It is easy to see where the story of Mary Howe of Damariscotta could have been confused with that of Mary Hart of New Haven over more than a century since their respective deaths.[3]

Another incident is that of a ghostly hitchhiker named "Mary," picked up by a young man on Davenport Avenue. After dropping her off at her residence, the man returned the next day to make sure she got in safely. He was told by the resident that nobody by that name lived at his address. The men then noticed that directly across the street stood Mary Hart's gravestone, in Evergreen Cemetery.

An entire cycle of supernatural legends surrounds consequences to persons who defy the curse by standing on Midnight Mary's grave at midnight. One tells of three friends who did just that. One of the friends told his buddies that Mary had been an accused witch (in the mid-1800s, no less!) who vowed to kill anyone who dared strike her grave at the stroke of midnight. Seven years later, one of the three friends had his throat ripped out at midnight on the anniversary of the incident. Seven years after that, the same occurred to another friend, etc.

Another interesting tale may be a corruption of a series of otherwise unrelated, yet historically true incidents. The legend says that three sailors, one at a time, went missing.

Their hats were later found on Midnight Mary's grave. According to the story, they had gone to Mary's grave but were frightened away. One never made out of the cemetery and got impaled on the iron spikes atop the fence. This tale was recorded from a teenage college student in 1972.

Now, three men *did* go missing way back in 1933, but they were certainly not sailors. They were escaped convicts from a prison in Dedham, Massachusetts named Bennie Pedato, Clarence DeCrane, and Charles Doherty. They escaped during a thunderstorm and fled in an automobile as far south as New Haven. Pedato and DeCrane were recaptured by New Haven police in a swamp behind Evergreen Cemetery, while Doherty continued to elude authorities.[4] Nobody was ever impaled on the Evergreen Cemetery spiked fence.

As for the clothing turning up on Mary's grave, this may also allude to an actual incident that occurred, something much more tragic than escaped inmates. In 1970, a little five-year-old New Haven girl, Jennifer Noon, went missing and was presumed kidnapped. Her clothing was found near St. Mary's Cemetery on Evergreen Avenue, though police refused to say if the articles showed signs of violence.[5]

The only *near* death that occurred at Evergreen Cemetery was an attempted suicide by a farmer's wife, Mrs. Lucius Smith, in 1897. She had taken carbolic acid in an attempt to poison herself over her daughter's grave, on Halloween night, October 31. Her husband arrived in time to prevent her immediate death and brought her to the hospital. She was presumably treated in time to save her life.[6]

And the ghost that frightens people away? That, too, may have a basis in fact. In December of 1939, Mr. and Mrs. Howard Landon came to Evergreen Cemetery in the evening to lay flowers on the grave of Mrs. Landon's deceased mother. They had lost track of time and found themselves in the cemetery after sundown. The caretaker had already padlocked the iron gates for the evening, unintentionally locking the couple within the high walls of the spiked iron fence. For over two hours, the couple shouted for help at passing "youngsters," who fled in terror from the "ghosts." Eventually, they were discovered by the caretaker's daughter, who notified her father and freed the Landons. The incident made page four of the *Hartford Courant*. The Landons swore that at least eight young people had fled from their shouts. Who knows how many times their ghost story was told to friends, retold, and embellished over nearly seventy years?[7]

Various other accounts of strange deaths and disappearances surround Midnight Mary's grave, and the people who dared trod upon it at the "witching hour." Unfortunately, direct evidence linking Mary's grave to these unfortunate events, or actual eyewitness testimony, is scarce. Still, who knows?

Can They All Be Wrong?

A much better documented, though less well known, accusation of premature burial occurred in seaside Connecticut. In August of 1905, seventeen-year-old Minnie Bedner died of gas asphyxiation at her home. She was a Hungarian immigrant working as a servant girl in Bridgeport's east side. When her family went to place flowers on her grave at St. Augustine's Cemetery (now located adjacent to the old Remington Factory), they clearly heard young Minnie calling to them in her native tongue! A crowd of local Hungarian immigrants soon gathered and, growing increasingly agitated, demanded of the undertaker that she be instantly exhumed. The undertaker declared that he could not dig up the body without the necessary permit but, "promised to get one tomorrow and open the grave for an investigation." The record, however, is silent as to whether the promised exhumation ever took place.[8]

On Thursday 16 August 2007, I took a trip to St. Augustine's Cemetery in Bridgeport. Not an easy place to find, it is located adjacent to the old Remington factory (itself believed to be haunted). Unfortunately, the old cemetery is

St. Augustine's Cemetery in Bridgeport where young Minnie
Bedner was reportedly buried alive. Her family heard her voice
calling to them in her native Hungarian tongue while they stood
at her grave.

badly overgrown and heavily vandalized. Even after a thorough search, I was unable to find Minnie Bedner's headstone. Most of the stones are flat, even with the earth, rather than the more common raised tombstones of other cemeteries. These flat memorials are almost entirely overgrown with grass and weeds, most of them have disappeared from view. More disturbing is the graffiti and litter that mark this forgotten and abandoned place. If Minnie Bedner still speaks from her grave, her words are lost in the bustle of urban society that surround the graveyard.

Perhaps someday this quiet place will receive the attention it deserves, a caretaker assigned, the necessary yard work done to uncover the overgrown stones, and we will once again know Minnie Bedner's resting place. One can only hope.

Chapter 5
The Essex Rappings

For eight days in January of 1915, a pretty blond seventeen-year-old girl threw the town of Essex into turmoil. Believers proclaimed her a medium who channeled the spirit of a dead man haunting the house where she lived, while skeptics accused her of perpetrating an elaborate hoax. The haunting of her adopted home in Essex lasted from Friday 15 January through Friday 22 January, during which time prophecies were made and fulfilled and spirit communications amazed hundreds of curious visitors at the home. Throughout the week long haunting, events at the Brown House in Essex were chronicled daily in the *Hartford Courant*, where they consistently made front page news. Debate between believers and skeptics divided the town of Essex and its surrounding communities in Deep River, Ivoryton, and Old Saybrook.

It all began the preceding summer, with the death of a widow, Mrs. Catherine T. Brown, at age sixty-two. Her son David had died twenty-six years prior, at age sixteen, leaving only a daughter, Mrs. Pitrillion of Lima, Ohio, to inherit her house. Mrs. Pitrillion had married and moved away to Ohio with her husband some time ago, but returned to Essex to be at her mother's deathbed. A Mrs. Rose Brooks, who nursed Mrs. Brown in the final stages of her illness, would later tell newspapermen that she had heard a strange, loud knocking in the house at the time of the widow's death. Mrs. Brooks and Mrs. Pitrillion thought the knockings to be coming from a maple tree outside the house. None of the women suspected that on 26 July 1914, while Mrs. Catherine T. Brown drew her last breath in this world, that the loud knockings might, in fact, be the spirit of her son, young "Davey" Brown, trying to communicate with the living in his mother's final moments.

Legend says that Mrs. Catherine T. Brown left a written will, though many later disputed this claim and no proof of a will was ever brought forward. By the time the haunting began, Mrs. Pitrillion had returned to Ohio and was unavailable for comment. According to the legend, the widow made a stipulation in the will that her house never be sold or rented.

In any case, will or no will, Mrs. Pitrillion did decide to let the house before returning to her husband in Ohio. She took pity on another widow with the last name of Brown, though of no relation to the Essex Browns, who was in dire need of a home for herself and five sons. Perhaps the widow, a Mrs. Charles Brown, originally of Middletown, reminded Mrs. Pitrillion of her own mother. This may well have been the case, since Mrs. Pitrillion worked out a very generous agreement with the widow, whereby she and her sons could live in the house rent free, at least until Mrs. Pitrillion succeeded in finding a buyer for the place. Mrs. Charles Brown and her sons were moved into the Essex house by September of 1914.[1]

One of the sons, William Brown, married May Wood of Stony Creek. The Brown newlyweds would also move to the Essex home. They were followed by May's teenage sister, Edna, when her father became horribly crippled and disfigured in a quarry explosion, leaving him unable to support his family. Seventeen-year-old Edna Wood, described as pretty, blond, petite and vivacious, seemed to have been held in very high esteem by the Browns. She bonded most strongly with Charles Brown, Jr., the youngest son, who was also seventeen. The Browns became especially protective of young Edna Wood, and did not allow her to speak to strangers.

The two teenagers may have had something else in common besides their age. While Edna Wood later claimed to be able to communicate and summon spirits, Charles

Brown said he could "see ghosts." If this were true, by modern terminology that would make Edna a clairaudient and clairsentient, while Charles would have been clairvoyant. The specific spirit that the family claimed to be haunting the home, that of sixteen-year-old David (or "Davey") Brown who died twenty-seven years ago, probably also was not an accident. Many paranormal professionals would agree that it is not at all unusual for a haunting spirit to seek out living persons its own "age" and temperament to communicate with. In death, as in life, teenagers enjoy being around other teenagers.

According to the Brown family, the ghostly communications began on Friday 15 January. Loud rappings were heard in the house by Edna Wood, and her brother-in-law, William Brown, went to the door to investigate, but found no one outside. William and May's three-year-old child then began humming a tune. The rappings started beating in time to the tune. One family member commented, "That's a nice tune," and was answered by three sharp raps.

Suspecting a communicative spirit, another family member asked, "Do you mean yes?" Three raps answered. The family quickly worked out a system of communicating with the spirit whereby three knocks meant "yes" and two meant "no."

The family was unable to summon the spirit upon command, however. At least, not until they discovered that it would always appear when Edna crawled into her bed (actually a folding metal cot in the widow Brown's upstairs room), upon her back and with her hands folded neatly over her chest beneath the quilt. It would not appear as a visual manifestation, only with the rappings which at times sounded as if they came from a nearby closet, door, or wall. By careful questioning, the family was able to discover that the spirit haunting their home was Davey Brown and that his spirit had resided in the home for at least the past ten years.

They also learned that the spirit disliked profanity, and would bang loudly when someone grew frustrated and swore in its presence. It also seemed to have an affinity for the modern music of the time, particularly the popular British anthem "It's a Long Way to Tipperary," to which the spirit would beat rhythmically. When the family discovered that the spirit could guess the age of any speaker with uncanny accuracy, answer questions that only the speaker knew the answer to, and even make prophetic predictions about the near future, they began to tell their neighbors of these strange events.

Soon dozens, then eventually hundreds of neighbors and folk from nearby towns began arriving at the Brown home to speak with the spirit. Some came to have questions answered about deceased loved ones, some to have questions answered about their own future and many others to skeptically interrogate the "spirit" and examine the teenage "medium" in hopes of uncovering a hoax. All the while, young Edna Wood had to lay supine in her bed, her hands covered, for the communication to work. Usually, but not always, questions were answered by rappings. Other times, Edna herself answered verbally, on behalf of the spirit.

Almost immediately, skeptics hypothesized that Edna was surreptitiously banging upon her own bed, while her hands were concealed. They noticed too, that rappings seemed only to come from the closet door, walls, or floor very near to Edna's bed. As publicity surrounding the haunting swelled, so too did the debate about its authenticity.

The *Hartford Courant* began covering the haunting, but almost immediately confusion surrounded the events, as seen in constant corrections appearing in each new article. For starters, some reporters were clearly confused about the two entirely separate Brown families and how each figured into the story. Also, initial reports were apparently taken from local gossip, not actual interviews with the family, resulting in confusion about which spirit actually haunted the home.

The first article to appear claimed that the spirit was that of the home's previous owner, Mrs. Catherine Brown, and that she had returned from the grave because the stipulations in her will had not been carried out. It was later discovered that there probably had never been a will at all, and the family adamantly denied that the deceased Mrs. Brown had been the haunting spirit, stating emphatically that it was instead her son, David. Early reports also claimed that Edna had begun hearing rappings upon the death of her father, Joseph Wood of Stoney Creek, when in fact Edna's father was not dead at all. Some articles confused the names of the two widows, Mrs. Catherine Brown (dead) and Mrs. Charles Brown (living), further muddying the waters.

Some less than tactful persons, including reporters, also challenged the veracity of the Browns based solely on the fact that the family lived in poverty and was largely illiterate (only two of the family members could read and write). "Political correctness," as we know it, did not exist in 1915. Even believers were quoted as having said of the Browns that they were "illiterate and somewhat shiftless" and that they "wouldn't have the brains to think up such a scheme or play it through." Some saw a fabricated haunting as a means for the Browns to discourage potential buyers of the house, allowing them to live there indefinitely. There may have been some truth to this, even if the haunting was legitimate and the Browns had consciously decided to exploit the haunting to keep their home.

From the hoax seekers, much was made of the fact that Edna's hands remained covered while the rappings transpired. To them, this fact was considered more definitive evidence of a hoax than the accuracy of the spirit's answers to questions put forward. If Edna were truly a medium, however, such a fact would have been immaterial. A spirit successfully channeled through a medium's body may use the body to communicate however it knows how. Therefore, even if it were Edna's physical hands that created some or all of the rappings, this in itself would not necessarily invalidate the possibility of a genuine haunting.

In the interests of unraveling the truth of events which transpired nearly a century ago, let us then examine the available evidence; the accuracy of predictions and prophecies made by the "spirit rappings" and Edna herself, as well as answers to questions asked of it.

It was reported that the spirit successfully guessed the ages of everyone who interviewed it. Of course, one must take into account the possibility that a skillful con artist could slowly knock out the raps, stopping only once the gullible questioner gasped out, "That's it!"

More interesting is the prophecy told an Adams Express agent at Essex, named Vernon E. Mather. When he asked how many packages he would receive on Friday, twenty-four distinct raps was his answer. On the next day, he told the *Courant*, he received twenty-four packages.

Dr. Charles D. Tyler, at one of the séances, was told by the rappings his age, fifty-five years, and also the dates of death of his father and mother. The spirit also told Dr. Tyler that he would collect a sum of $8 the next day. According to Dr. Tyler, the spirit had been accurate to within three cents. A Mrs. Roscoe Doane was also converted to belief by the accuracy of the rappings, but would later recant when it looked like the majority of her neighbors scoffed at her belief. A Burton S. Clapp was told a prophecy that his horse would fall sick within a week and die within ten days. Unfortunately, no record survives of what befell Mr. Clapp's horse.

Among the most vehement of Edna Wood's supporters were local men Stephen W. Doane, Barney Young, Robert Davis, and Richard Ferranti. Barney insisted not only that the rappings were spiritual in nature, but also that he felt a spectral hand press down on his shoulder while in the house.

"I know there's no fake about it," he said. "I talked with the spirit, and, what's more, I felt it. I was a-sitting in the bedroom while the rappings were going on, and all of a sudden, while it was giving me an answer to a question I had asked, I felt a hand take hold of my shoulder and press down on it. I looked around and by gosh there wasn't anyone there at all. If that wasn't the spirit, I want to know what it was."

Stephen Doane, an employee of Essex doctor Charles B. Tyler, agreed that "there's something about this thing that ought to be explained before anybody starts calling it a fake." The spirit not only told him how old he was (fifty), but also how old he had been when his mother died (three) and how old he had been when his father died (seventeen). Doane insisted that, "there isn't a soul in town that knew it until then." Amusingly, the spirit had also successfully told a man named Earl D. Hillsinger that he had four bottles of beer hidden in his wagon outside the house. Barney Young recalled, "Yes, and Hillsinger got up and left the room, saying he was afraid somebody would swipe them when it was known they were there."[2]

One interesting statement by Edna Wood on the spirit's behalf would have definitively proven or disproven her veracity, if the historical record could have been more complete. She was asked to solve a mystery—what had become of John Dolph, an Essex resident that had gone missing ten years ago. Edna answered that John Dolph had gone out West, where he had been murdered by five men, but that his body had been brought back to Essex and buried.

Unraveling the mystery of John Dolph is difficult, since the historical record is incomplete. There is no record of a John Dolph in the census records for Essex, or any other known account. There is, however, a Jonas Dolph (first name has also been spelled as Johas, Janes and James, in various accounts), husband to Emily Dolph, who appears in the 1880, 1900, 1910, and 1920 censuses. His name is the only one even approximating a "John Dolph;" no other Dolphs even have a "J" for a middle initial. If Jonas were indeed the John that Edna referred to, then he was still alive and well in 1920 and does not appear to have gone missing at all, since he also appeared in the 1910 census, only five years before events at the Brown House. It is certainly possible that a Dolph relative named John may have been staying with Jonas and Emily and went missing, but until further documentary evidence is brought to light, it is impossible to say for certain. This particular mystery, along with Burton Clapp's horse, may never be solved.

Meanwhile, seventeen-year-old Charles Brown, Jr. had an otherworldly experience of his own in the woods outside their house. He claimed to have seen "a man in black and a woman in white" in the act of burying something in a nearby field, but was too frightened to investigate after dark. Family members later dug in the area where he saw the ghosts and uncovered some "old clothing" and "some hair." An uncovered cap was believed to be fairly new and recently buried.

One of the spirit's most interesting predictions was also its last; that it would go away for a time, but would return on 10 February. This prediction, however, appears to have never come true since the Brown House haunting came to a screeching halt on the night of Friday 22 January, when two visiting women exposed the entire "hoax."

The women credited with this skillful act of debunking were a Mrs. Frank Torrey of Essex and Mrs. Harriet Hefflon of Old Saybrook. The Brown family told a very different version of the events of that night, namely that Mrs. Hefflon "stole" the ghost and took it back to Old Saybrook with her.

It happened like this.

Crowds of nearly 100 curious visitors, skeptics, and believers occupied the house into the late hours. Many asked questions and were answered by the rappings while Edna Wood lay in her bed under her quilt. Mrs. Torrey and Mrs. Hefflon were also in attendance. Mrs. Torrey, though a student and believer of Spiritualism, came to the Brown House with an eye to debunk the Essex haunting, if possible. Mrs. Hefflon came for much the same purpose and decided to concentrate her attention on young Edna Wood, watching her closely for signs of trickery.

As various questions were answered by the mysterious rappings, Mrs. Torrey at one point demanded that Edna put her hands above the quilt in plain sight. According to Mrs. Torrey, Edna placed first one, then the other hand in sight, with apparent reluctance. At that point, when the rappings continued, Mrs. Torrey swore they had been caused by Frank Brown while standing behind Edna's bed.

"Yes, I heard the rapping," she accused Frank Brown, "and I saw you tapping the floor with your foot."

Edna, meanwhile, seemed to suffer adversely under Mrs. Hefflon's continued staring. Apparently frightened, the girl leapt out of her bed, accused Mrs. Hefflon of trying to mesmerize her and fled downstairs. As the family tried to console Edna Wood, she declared that "that woman," Mrs. Hefflon, had "stolen" the spirit of Davey Brown away, to take with her to Old Saybrook.

Mrs. Hefflon later told the *Courant* that she had not tried to hypnotize the girl and that she did not even know how to hypnotize a person. "If there were any spirits in the house," she quipped, "they were of the fiery sort."[3]

For days and nights following, hundreds of people came to the Brown House, only to be turned away by the Brown family. The ghost is gone, they were told, stolen away by a woman mesmerist from Old Saybrook.

It would never return.

The *Hartford Courant* printed an article entitled "ESSEX 'SPIRIT' EXPOSED BY TWO WOMEN, GIRL IN BED MADE THE RAPS, BOY HELPED." That would have seemed to make an end of the matter, but not everyone was convinced. Debate continued in the quiet little town of Essex, as neighbors argued vehemently with each other. Interest in the matter was not nearly so quick to die down, and so the newspaper decided to do a more in-depth expose.

A 30 January article entitled "ESSEX GIRL WHO LOST A GHOST" featured a full length picture of pretty, teenage Edna Wood, complete with what appears to be an apron and bonnet. Her sister, May, was quoted as saying,

"Mrs. Hefflon took the ghost away with her. She said she was going to do it and she did. We hope she keeps it."

The Brown family had apparently not anticipated the amount of publicity the affair generated, the stress put upon them, as well as the sneering judgment of their neighbors was unexpected and unappreciated. Edna Wood, too, expressed the stress of her experience and relief that it was finally over. May and Edna, together with May's husband, William Brown, left the house to stay with the girls' father, James Wood.[4] The cot where Edna had made her "spirit contacts" was folded up and passed along to one Niles E. Gladding of Middle Cove, where it was stored for safe keeping. A "For Sale" sign appeared on the property. Mrs. Pitrillion had decided to sell the property after all, perhaps she, too, had tired of the unwanted publicity surrounding the innocuous seeming two-story house.[5]

Noted spiritualist May Vanderbilt, while giving a lecture at a Connecticut spiritualist meeting, was asked about the recent news coverage concerning the Essex rappings. Asked: "Was the first or last article on the Essex ghost in 'The Courant' true and why do the papers give such reports against spiritualism?" She replied that "newspapers are more a popular reflector than a righteous educator." She went on:

"Down in your little town of Essex they claim to have an apparition... If that little Brown girl is a station for receiving messages from the spirit world, it makes no difference how ignorant she may be... on the other hand, if it is not true, it is up to the spiritualists of Connecticut to prove it false. I am inclined to believe that the little girl is a medium."[6]

The prophesied date of 10 February came and went, with no return of the spirit. Edna was gone, the bed was gone, and the house soon to be sold. Not missing a beat, the *Hartford Courant* published the expected article on 11 February, still page one news, entitled "ESSEX SPIRITS FAIL TO SAVE BROWN HOME."

This much is true, but was the prophecy untrue? Nowhere that the spirit's last prophecy appears is a year attached to the date of 10 February. So keep that in mind, if you find yourself traveling the old Meadow Woods district of Essex, where the Brown House once stood, in the month of February.

And if you hear a strange rapping you cannot account for, or a mysterious man in black or woman in white deep in the woods, burying some unknown articles... it may be best if you just continue on your way...

Chapter 6
The Bridgeport Poltergeist

The Lindley Street address of the famous Bridgeport Poltergeist incident of 1974, believed to have inspired Spielberg's film. (The home is now privately owned and occupied. Please respect trespassing laws.)

Few instances of poltergeist activity have ever been so well documented or have enjoyed so many credible witnesses as the phenomena that occurred in 1974 on Bridgeport's Lindley Street. Flying furniture, inexplicable pounding noises, and violent attacks by invisible forces were all witnessed by professional police officers, firemen, newspaper and radio reporters, Roman Catholic priests, friends, and neighbors of the afflicted family. None of these witnesses ever recanted their testimony as to what they witnessed during those fateful few days in late November, even under enormous pressure from their superiors to do so.

It began in a little one-story bungalow, with a middle-aged couple, Gerard and Laura Goodin. Their one biological child, a son, had died in 1967, after which they adopted little three-year-old Marcia, a Canadian Indian girl. The Goodins had a great affection for their adopted daughter and were protective of her, almost to a fault. An intelligent, introspective child, she had a brilliant imagination and remarkable charisma. By the time she was ten, she had convinced her devoted, over-protective parents that "Sam," the family cat, could in fact talk, even though everyone else who witnessed this phenomena could clearly see the girl was an amateur ventriloquist.

Talking cat aside, events surrounding young Marcia, or "Marcy" as her family knew her, eventually drew the attention of nationwide press as she became the epicenter of "classic" and extraordinarily violent poltergeist activity. Before delving into the incredible events of November, 1974, a brief explanation of poltergeist phenomenon is probably appropriate.

The word "poltergeist" is German for "noisy ghost." The phenomenon is very different from the Spielberg movie of the same name and has nothing to do with graveyards or the spirits of dead folk. Most researchers and investigators in the paranormal field agree that a poltergeist is something very different from spirits and ghosts, and is an invisible force created, or summoned, by a living person who has suffered traumatic events or significant emotional disturbance. This person is commonly referred to as the "epicenter" upon which the phenomenon revolves, and is generally an adolescent, usually but not always a young girl. About half the "experts" in this sort of phenomenon believe the epicenter creates the poltergeist itself, through latent psychokinetic abilities of which the child is herself unaware. Others claim that the poltergeist is really an entity from beyond our reality, or dimension, summoned unconsciously by the child through repressed, severe physical, or emotional trauma. In this second theory, the epicenter serves as a conduit through which the entity briefly enters our own realm to cause what mischief it can. Sexual abuse is sometimes, but not always, believed to be a factor.

The child who serves as the epicenter often fits a "type." He or she is usually just entering puberty, has above average intelligence, is introverted and lonely, imaginative, and closed off from normal social interactions, either by choice or by overprotective or controlling parents. Often, the epicenter has self-destructive feelings, which the poltergeist tries to act out by attacking the very person, the epicenter, which brought it into being. There is some debate as to whether a poltergeist has any actual intelligence of its own, though most agree that it becomes progressively more powerful as it generates more fear and negative emotion in a household. Poltergeists are generally limited to one household and family, and hauntings by poltergeists are usually brief, in comparison to those by ghosts or spirits. A poltergeist haunting may last anywhere from a few days to a few months (though supernatural events leading up to the haunting may take place years before), whereas ghostly hauntings have been known to last for centuries when conditions are right. Hauntings by poltergeists are often much more dramatic, however, involving noises like a rapping or pounding on doors or walls, forcefully moving and throwing objects, either at persons or seemingly at random, and slapping, pinching or otherwise attacking the epicenter, persons of central significance to the epicenter, or persons who simply get in the way. As a poltergeist gains power through fear and negative emotions of the inhabitants of a household, it may gain the ability to manifest auditory phenomenon such as whispers, groans, howls or even short sentences (usually reflecting the subconscious emotions of the epicenter). It may also manifest visually for brief times, in forms human-like or monstrous, perhaps representing the subconscious fears of the epicenter. Poltergeist hauntings often end as suddenly as they begin, though why this might be nobody seems to know.

According to the Goodins, strange bangings and pounding began in the house in 1972 and continued for the next two years, until the remarkable events of 1974. Inspectors of the house assured the Goodins at the time that there was nothing structurally wrong with it. It should be noted, however, that heavy construction at nearby St. Vincent's Hospital was going on during that time, even though none of the Goodins' neighbors made complaints.

In the summer of 1974, a disembodied hand appeared in front of a window. Then, in early fall, Laura Goodin heard three distinct knocks on her front door. When she answered, no one was about, but she saw three "wet footprints" on the otherwise dry ground outside. These relatively minor events were just a prelude, however, to the chaos that enveloped their little home in late November.

The haunting of 966 Lindley Street began in earnest on Thursday 21 November of 1974. At 4:30 pm, while the family of three was eating dinner in the kitchen, they heard the window in the front room shatter. Gerard Goodin ran to investigate and found that the window had been smashed from the inside. Nobody else was in the home at the time. The next afternoon, on Friday 22 November, around 4:00 pm, the curtains in the front room suddenly fell from the wall. Things quickly escalated afterward.

The Goodins returned from a day trip to New York on Saturday 23 November, at around 5:00 pm to find their home a shambles. A portable television had been moved, dishes began flying about the house and shattering on the kitchen floor, religious articles seemed to leap off the walls and fall to the floor. They also watched stunned as their 350-pound refrigerator lifted up off the floor before settling back down, and the kitchen television toppled over of its own accord. Worse, the terrible poundings sounded worse than ever and continued until midnight.

At 8:00 am the following morning, Sunday 24 November, chairs and tables began turning over on their own, waking the frightened family. They called their neighbors, the Hofmanns, who hurried over and themselves witnessed the portable television in the kitchen begin rocking back and forth. Another neighbor, an off duty policeman named Holsworth, was summoned to the house and saw the refrigerator lift up again, turn and drop to the floor with a loud thud. A knife holder in the kitchen flew at Gerard Goodin, which he caught.

Neighbor Hofmann wasted no time in calling well known demonologists Ed and Lorraine Warren in Monroe. For his part, neighbor Holsworth phoned his on-duty friends in Bridgeport Police Department. Bridgeport Police Officers Joseph Tomek, Carl Leonzi, George Wilson, and Leroy Lawson responded to the scene as the ruckus began to draw a crowd outside the house. All BPD Officers observed the refrigerator, portable TV, furniture and objects rise, fall, spin, or otherwise move without any action on the part of the home's occupants. Patrolman Tomek noted all of this in his official police report (File #74-79962), to Bridgeport Police Captain Charles Baker.[1]

Police Sergeant Mangaiamele arrived on the scene shortly afterward, with Bridgeport Fire Chief Zwierlien and several city firemen. These credible witnesses also were shocked to see with their own eyes furniture moving and falling about the house. Some member of the family decided to contact the local parish priest, Father Doyle, who also responded and witnessed the same phenomena. Fire Chief Zwierlien claimed "witchcraft" to be the cause. Father Doyle performed a blessing on the house and left shortly afterward, during a period of relative calm.

The Warrens arrived that afternoon, followed shortly by Roman Catholic priest William Charbonneau, a personal friend whom they had contacted. Arriving also with the Warrens was a twenty-one-year-old seminary student named

Paul Eno (who's narrative of the events of the Bridgeport Poltergeist probably remain the best contemporary written account to date). By that time, crowds had gathered on both sides of Lindley Street, and Laura Goodin had just returned from a brief trip to St. Vincent's Hospital after the portable television had fallen on her foot, breaking her toe. Little Marcy was interrogated in the basement of the home by a newly arrived team of Bridgeport police investigators, who listened incredulously to her account of the talking cat, Sam. They were skeptical of the entire affair, not having personally witnessed any of the phenomena in the home and already some of them had begun to declare the entire thing a hoax. After a blessing by Father Charbonneau, the investigators departed, leaving only a handful of patrolmen to control the crowd outside, which had by then grown to over 500 spectators.

Father Charbonneau and Eno both interviewed Marcy, whom the Warrens already suspected as the epicenter of the supernatural activity taking place. They declared the happenings to be the work of a poltergeist. Reporters arrived afterward to interview Father Charbonneau, Eno, the Warrens, and the Goodins. While these reporters were conducting their interview, a large dresser in Marcy's room was thrown across the room to smash into her closet door.

By 8:00 pm, the crowd outside the Goodin home had grown to several thousand onlookers. The story by then had received nationwide attention, reported in the Associated Press, United Press International and Reuters, as well as other broadcasting networks. At 9:30 pm, while Father Charbonneau was talking with Marcy in her bedroom, a large bureau flew across the room. At 11:00 pm, a television fell on Eno's leg, wounding him slightly.

In the early morning hours of Monday 25 November, around 8:00 am, the Roman Catholic Diocese of Bridgeport, which had ignored requests by Father Charbonneau and the Warrens for an exorcism, released its official statement on the Lindley Street haunting. A spokesman for the diocese stated that it was the position and opinion of the Church Diocese that the phenomena in Bridgeport were the result of "natural causes." No further support or help from the church would be forthcoming.[2]

Media at that time declared the crowd outside to number around 10,000. Some of the more emotional onlookers loudly declared that the Apocalypse was nigh.

Later that afternoon, the house became suddenly flooded with a foul fetid odor that had no visible cause. John Sopko, a reporter for the Bridgeport Post, was on scene and witnessed the event. The odor dissipated, then returned hours later.

At 7:10 pm, Marcy was thrown bodily across the room by an invisible source. At Eno's urging, all occupants temporarily fled the house. Later, after the family reentered their home and two reporters from WNAB Radio arrived for an interview, a mirror in Marcy's room fell to the floor and a kitchen table overturned twice. More furniture and objects were tossed about, and at one point, the chair in which Marcy was sitting began to lift into the air with her seated upon it.

Throughout all this, the terrified family and their well-meaning guests did all they could to shield Marcy from harm. It became increasingly obvious, however, that the poltergeist activity seemed centered upon the little girl and around her bedroom. The Warrens and Eno left that night, promising to return the following afternoon.

After they left, however, a fresh team of Bridgeport Police arrived on the scene and had a lengthy private discussion with Gerard and Laura Goodin. At the same time, professional interrogators secluded Marcy and got her to "confess" that the entire thing was a hoax that she had perpetrated. The Goodins cannot rightly be blamed for what followed, after all they wanted their lives back and feared how the unwanted publicity might affect little Marcy.

When the Warrens and Eno tried to return, as promised, they were refused admittance by the Goodins, who actually had policemen remove Eno from the property. Family lawyers threatened the Warrens not to go public in interviews about events in their house.

Tuesday, 26 November, Bridgeport Police Superintendent Joseph Walsh released an official statement to the press. He announced that the Lindley Street affair was a hoax played upon a gullible populace by a lonely little girl. He went on to say that "There are no ghosts in Bridgeport," and that all persons claiming to have witnessed unexplainable phenomenon (including his own police officers and Bridgeport firemen) were "victims of the power of suggestion."

This position was not supported by Bridgeport Police Lieutenant Leonard Cocco, who backed his officers. He went on record with the media, saying of the original patrolmen at the scene, "Together they have more than 100 years of experience... if they said they saw something, they saw something."

The battle lines were clearly drawn. The Bridgeport Police Chief implied that the Warrens were tricksters who had played upon an emotionally and psychologically fragile family's superstitions. The Warrens insisted the Bridgeport Police Chief covered up the truth in the interests of restoring order in the neighborhood. Fire Chief John Gleason, who had been to the house, declared that, "Dinner plates started rattling, pictures were jumping off the wall, a TV fell over and a big heavy leather chair jumped at least six inches off the floor."

Despite the official position of the Bridgeport Diocese (none of whom set foot in the house), Father Charbonneau never recanted his account of having a television and chest fall over. He bravely defied the Church hierarchy and publicly declared, "They were not caused by natural means, I saw nothing that would make me think it was a hoax."

Bridgeport radio newsman Tim Quinn, along with numerous other reporters who had personally witnessed the phenomena, also questioned the veracity of Chief Walsh's statement of a hoax. Quinn insisted that he saw little Marcy get slammed against a wall five feet away, "like someone had a rope on her and pulled her into the wall."

Nonpartisan reporters, in an attempt to ascertain the truth of the matter, interviewed professional magicians to determine if, in fact, a ten-year-old girl could perpetuate such incredible acts by subterfuge. Professional magician Malcolm Ryder of Windsor Locks stated that such a magical act "could be done" but "for a 10-year-old girl to pull this, with other people in the room watching... I'd have a terrible time doing that myself."

Terms like "mass hysteria" and "mass delusion" were bandied about. Perhaps most insightful was an interview of Dr. George Allen, associate professor of Psychology at UCONN, reported in the *Hartford Courant*. As to the powers of suggestion, in relation to the events on Lindley Street, he said that supposed witnesses may have been fooled "if people bought the explanation." He went on to say, however, that science does not yet have all the answers to the untapped potential of the human mind, and that Marcia may have had unusual power over objects or persons.[3]

More than a decade after the events of 1974, Ed Warren was interviewed about the Bridgeport poltergeist. When asked about the police chief's declaration of a hoax, he explained, "Most of us just don't want to face the supernatural... here were are, a nation that seems to believe deeply in some sort of life beyond this one, yet we don't want to believe that that life might have any effect on our current existence."[4]

There are few left who can provide us with fresh insight into the events of the 1974 Bridgeport Poltergeist. The

Goodins have both been dead for years. Marcia, after undergoing psychiatric treatment on the insistence of her parents, has disappeared into obscurity somewhere. Many of the credible police, firemen, priests, reporters, and neighbors who were witnesses of the events have been censured by their superiors or co-workers, their credibility questioned by those who were never there, or are themselves no longer among the living. The most telling fact about these incredibly diverse professionals who witnessed the Bridgeport Poltergeist, however, is not their current silence on the matter... but that none of them ever recanted their original testimonies.

This fact alone speaks volumes.

Chapter 7
The Lighthouse Keepers
New London Ledge Light

New London's Ledge Light, believed to be haunted by "Ernie," a former lighthouse keeper who leapt from the roof when his wife left him for a ferryboat captain.

New London Ledge Light is unique among Connecticut's lighthouses, not only for its unusual architectural style and history but also for the persistent legend of its haunting. Its resident spirit, most often referred to as "Ernie," has become the most famous lighthouse ghost in the Northeast. His story is told and retold, with several variations, by tour guides, folklorists, Coast Guardsmen, paranormal investigators, and others. Even old time New Londoners, skeptical of ghosts and hauntings in general, cherish the legend of Ernie, as an integral part of town lore.

Architecturally, New London Ledge Light (or just "Ledge Light," for short) is a marvel. Located at the entrance to New

London harbor, where the Thames River meets Long Island Sound, it looks more like an elegant red brick mansion with a lantern cupola atop, than a typical lighthouse. It sits about a mile offshore from Ocean Beach Park upon the underwater Southwest Ledge, at the extreme eastern end of Long Island Sound. Completed in 1909 by Hamilton R. Douglas Company of New London at a total cost of $93,968.96, its style reflected the architecture of wealthy homeowners in New London, boasting a mansard roof and paired windows in the French Second Empire style. It must have looked right at home with its shore-bound neighbors in New London harbor, until the hurricane of 1938 destroyed them all. Originally named "Southwest Ledge Light," the name was quickly changed to avoid confusion with an identically named lighthouse of New Haven.

The station began operation on 10 November 1909, and was attended by a keeper and two assistants. Keepers would continue its operation until the Coast Guard took over in 1939, with two- and three-man crews who lived at the lighthouse. These would later grow to four-man crews, with a three-man relief, until the place became automated in 1987. Ledge Light has remained unoccupied since its automation.[1]

The mansion-style red brick and granite building is surmounted by an octagonal brick watchroom which supports the cast-iron cylindrical lantern. The light was originally a fourth order Fresnel lens, manufactured in Paris, which now sits in the Custom House Museum of Maritime History in New London. The lighthouse was the last on Long Island Sound to become automated, when the lens was replaced with a modern VRB-25 optic. The loss of the original lens prompted one nostalgic Coast Guardsman to lament, "When you replace that light, you've taken the heart out of the lighthouse."

Though most trace the legend of Ledge Light's haunting to the death of a mysterious lighthouse keeper of the 1920s or 1930s, at least one source claims that supernatural happenings began much earlier, during the lighthouse's construction.

Brae Rafferty, a marine biologist of the New London Ledge Lighthouse Foundation and Project Oceanology, said, "Over the years I've heard a lot of stories… things that go bump in the night. I've heard that even when they were building it, unexplained things were going on."[2]

In a conversation between Rafferty and a woman whose grandfather had worked construction on the lighthouse, the woman told of paranormal phenomena that began even before the lighthouse was completed. Workmen complained of missing tools, unnatural sounds, and weird, supernatural shadows.[3]

The most commonly repeated legend, however, is that of "Ernie." With slight variations, depending on the source, the legend goes like this. Sometime in the 1920s or 1930s, Ledge Light had a keeper named Ernie, or possibly "George." His real name is unknown. Ernie married a young woman half his age, who lived in their home on New London's shore. Apparently, the loneliness of a lighthouse keeper's wife was too much for her, so she ran off with another man, the captain of the Block Island ferry. Ernie received his last letter from his wife, telling him of her abandonment, while he was working his shift at the lighthouse. Consumed with despair, Ernie either committed suicide by leaping from the lighthouse roof or (according to some) drank himself into a stupor and fell to his death.

Despite the fact that no historical record survives of an "Ernie" ever having been keeper of Ledge Light, the legend blossomed during the period from 1939 until 1987 when Coast Guardsmen began to notice several phenomena with no natural explanation. Among the events attributed by the Guardsmen to Ernie are the making of noises (particularly ghostly footsteps), opening and closing doors, turning the television or foghorn on and off, decks that swabbed themselves, and secured boats being set adrift.

"I've never gone through a two-week period when I haven't had an experience with Ernie," Coast Guardsman

Jerry Sutters told the *Hartford Courant* in 1978. He went on to explain that faulty wiring could not be the cause of the phenomena, since the lighthouse's wiring had been checked and "found to be in good order." Also, footsteps in the middle of the night (when most of the phenomena seem to have occurred) could not be caused by the house settling, since it sits on a foundation of solid concrete.

Terry Wilson, a fireman apprentice stationed with Sutters, agreed. He related how the foghorn had turned on and off by "someone or something other than the two men stationed there" and how the light at the top of the lighthouse, run by gears and a weight, had gone off unexpectedly.

Sutters' wife reportedly had seen the keeper's specter during one of her visits. After seeing Ernie's "shadow," she was so badly spooked that she refused to come out to the lighthouse again.[4]

It is interesting to note that only women seem to be capable of seeing Ernie's ghost. Coast Guard officer in charge Randy Watkins related a similar experience in the 1980s, in which his wife, Lucretia, had spent the night with him in the lighthouse's master bedroom. She had awakened when the door opened and had "the eerie feeling of someone in the room, staring."

So common is the belief in Ernie among the Coast Guardsmen that dissenting skeptics are few. In 1984, one officer in charge, Tim Grant, tried to dispel some of the legend by stating that he did not believe any of the dozens of stories he had heard from previous Guardsmen assigned the post. "I haven't seen or heard anything unexplained," he said, "None of the crew has, either." Grant, however, went on to explain that he had only been assigned to Ledge Light a little over a year ago and that "We've got a fairly new crew."

Grant's opinion was apparently not shared by several of the last Coast Guardsman to oversee the automation process of the 1980s. The crew claimed that Ernie had become agitated by the automation of the lighthouse. Guardsman

Charles Kerr found that papers on his desk had rearranged themselves, while Paul Noke's bed apparently moved about the room by itself. Noke became so spooked by his moving bed that he took to sleeping on the couch. Automation was officially completed 1 May 1987. The last Coast Guardsman to leave recorded his final entry in the log:

> *Rock of slow torture. Ernie's domain. Hell on earth—may New London Ledge's light shine on forever because I'm through. I will watch it from afar while drinking a brew.*

Ernie's spirit is not the only one said to haunt Ledge Light.

Members of the New London Ledge Lighthouse Foundation, particularly marine biologist Brae Rafferty and treasurer Jerry Olson, have uncovered other strange happenings and accounts in their research. Rafferty tells of a shipwreck that occurred a decade before Ledge Light was built. The doomed ship went down at nearby Black Ledge, killing perhaps a dozen aboard. Apparently, witnesses at the time saw a young man, who successfully made it to shore, frantically search for his new bride. Grief stricken, he was seen to gradually enter the water and disappear forever.

Olson tells of a separate incident that may have occurred in 1913 or 1914, in which a sailboat containing a man, woman, and their daughter, capsized in the Sound during a fierce storm. According to local tradition, the lighthouse keeper saw the man and woman swimming desperately in the dead of night, and successfully brought them safely to the lighthouse. He was shocked and saddened to hear that their daughter had been lost in the storm. The next day, the keeper was astonished to find that the couple had vanished without a trace. Even more strange, visitors from shore told of having rescued a young girl, who told them a similar story in which her parents had been lost. The shore folk told the keeper that the girl had also disappeared the following morning, without explanation.

Either of these tales may explain enduring accounts of spirits observed in or around the lighthouse, always apparently searching for a loved one. Olson claims to have had a personal encounter with a female spirit he has dubbed "The Lady of the Ledge," in which he heard her distinctly clear her throat while his back was turned. He says that he saw a sudden image in his head of an attractive middle-aged woman. When he turned, however, the spirit had vanished.

For more than twenty years, paranormal personalities, investigators, mediums, and the like have visited Ledge Light and contributed their own tales to the cycle of lighthouse legends. "Ghost psychologist" Dr. Roger Pile and his wife, who acted as medium, claimed to make contact with the "real" spirit haunting Ledge Light in 1981. According to the Piles, the spirit was that of a keeper named John Randolph who had committed suicide by slashing his own throat with a knife, following an argument with his wife. Unfortunately, no record of a keeper named Randolph exists.

Another paranormal investigator claims that Ledge Light is a "vortex" of supernatural activity, centered upon the northeast corner. Her feeling is that whatever spirits remain are harmless and benign.

Most recently, Ledge Light was investigated by perhaps the most well known paranormal team since the Warrens. The Atlantic Paranormal Society (TAPS) investigated the lighthouse in 2005, for an episode televised on the Sci-Fi Channel's popular reality show, *Ghost Hunters*.[5]

The episode aired in August of 2005. Video evidence from their investigation, though labeled inconclusive by the team's founders, Grant Wilson and Jason Hawes, can be seen on DVD or from the popular TAPS website.[6]

Does Ernie's spirit remain? At least one historian and folklorist believes so. He writes; "His spirit doesn't talk and he has never harmed anyone but his energy force is strong. He appears at the top of stairs for a few seconds and then vanishes. When his spirit is present, scraping sounds, bumps and soft footsteps can be heard."[7]

Ledge Light is still open to the public for tours through the summer season. Project Oceanology runs the tours, and reservations must be made in advance. Check out the Project Oceanology website for details. A number of lighthouse cruise tours and fishing boats also pass by Ledge Light, as well as other well-known Connecticut lighthouses. These boats do not land, however, but for some of the most remote lighthouses, this is the best way to get good photographs of their exteriors. The best place to view Ledge Light from the shore is from the private beach on New London's Pequot Avenue, though you will need a good zoom lens for pictures.

Penfield Reef Light

Ledge Light is not the only haunted lighthouse along Connecticut's shore. Less well known, though equally well documented, is the legend of Penfield Reef Light's ghostly keeper. The Penfield legend has a more solid foundation in fact, beginning with the 1916 drowning death of its keeper, Fred A. Jordan.

Penfield Reef Light sits upon a shoal toward the western end of Long Island Sound, which extends a mile out from the beach at Fairfield. The area had been a particularly dangerous one to mariners and the site of many wrecks before the completion of the lighthouse in 1874. Its form is similar to Ledge Light and nearby Race Rock Light, in that it is a combination dwelling and tower, constructed of brick and granite. Like Ledge Light, an elegant mansard roof crowns the twenty-eight-foot-square dwelling, with octagonal watchroom topped by a cylindrical lantern. The two-story dwelling originally contained four bedrooms, a kitchen, living room, and oil room. The lantern held a fourth order Fresnel lens that flashed red at fifty-one feet above sea level, before that lens was replaced by the more modern VRB-25 optic.

Although Fred Jordan was not the first lighthouse keeper at Penfield, the legend of its haunting certainly begins with him. Wishing to spend Christmas ashore with his family, Keeper Jordan attempted to row to shore at Black Rock Harbor on the afternoon of 22 December 1916. He left Assistant Keeper Rudolph Iten in charge of Penfield Reef Light. Watching from the lighthouse, Iten was a helpless witness to the tragedy that followed.

Despite high seas and strong winds, Jordan felt the effort to join his family for the holiday well worth the risk. He barely made more than a hundred yards from the lighthouse when his boat capsized, about twenty minutes past noon. He signaled for Iten to come to his aid, which Iten tried desperately to do with a smaller boat, but by then the waves had become higher and increasingly rough. By the time Iten got the tiny boat going, it was 1:00 pm, and already too late for Jordan. Jordan had drifted a mile and a half away, to the southwest.

Newspapers reported the tragedy days later, even though Jordan's body would not be found for another three months. Jordan was thirty-five years old, with a wife and two children.[8]

Rudolph Iten replaced Jordan as head keeper, remaining in the position for the next ten years. He and his two assistants, Walter Harper and Arthur Bender, claimed to have witnessed ghostly manifestations of Fred Jordan on several occasions. When asked about these phenomena, the men often quoted an old saying that, "What the reef takes, the reef will give back."

The first reported manifestation took place only days after Jordan's death. Keeper Rudolph Iten was asleep during one of the worst storms of December 1916. One of his assistants was on duty. He awakened to a feeling that someone was in the room with him. He later recalled, "Sitting up I distinctly saw a gray, phosphorescent figure emerging from the room formerly occupied by Fred Jordan. It hovered at the top of the stairs, and then disappeared in the darkness below."[9]

Iten followed the figure downstairs, to where his log book lay open. The figure was gone, but the book lay open to the page on which Iten had transcribed the event of Jordan's drowning.

At least two other incidents are credited to the spirit of Fred Jordan. One is that of a yacht that ran into trouble on a nearby reef and was led to safety by a mysterious man in a rowboat, who afterward vanished. The second incident involved two youths, whose boat capsized. In danger of drowning, the two boys were rescued by a mysterious unknown man, who likewise vanished.[10]

Both of these accounts seem to originate from an undated newspaper article in the Bridgeport Public Library. The incident with the yacht probably refers to the 1953 explosion and sinking of the *Privateer II*, about two miles from Penfield Reef. The unidentified skipper was eventually rescued by Coast Guardsmen from the lighthouse.[11]

The incident with the two youths most likely refers to the rescue of teenagers James Janes and Richard Del Vetco in 1966. The boys were eventually rescued after their makeshift raft capsized, once they had been spotted by lobster fisherman Don Whittle, who contacted the Coast Guard.[12]

The specter of Fred Jordan has reportedly been seen flitting among the rocks, or leaning upon the rail surrounding the lantern. He has reportedly been seen among the jagged black rocks, swaying as if in agony. If the spirit of Fred Jordan does indeed haunt Penfield Reef, the haunting seems to be a benevolent one. In death, as in life, he continues to rescue endangered youths and yachtsmen, and to ensure that the all-important beacon shines to warn mariners traversing the Sound.

Penfield Reef Light is automated now, like the rest of its brethren, and vacant of living occupants. But whether the lighthouse is *entirely* vacant, is, of course, a matter of debate.

Chapter 8
Secret Deaths at Seaside

F ew places have a creepier, more morbid history than the old Seaside Sanatorium in Waterford. Located at 36 Shore Road, the grand Tudor Revival architecture of the former institution was designed by Cass Gilbert, an architect famous in his time for having also designed the Woolworth Building in New York and the U.S. Supreme Court building in Washington. Gilbert's architectural accomplishments in Connecticut include also Waterbury's City Hall and Union Station in New Haven.[1] Construction on the new Seaside Sanatorium compound was underway by the 1930s as a tuberculosis hospital for children, and by 1934, child patients were transferred to the Waterford location from the original Seaside Sanatorium at Crescent Beach, Niantic.[2]

The premise of the Sanatorium was to treat children stricken with TB by seeing they got as much sun and fresh air as possible. The Sanatorium was then administered by the State Tuberculosis Commission. The Seaside treatment method of sun and fresh air, known as the heliotropic treatment, was a fairly standard one, until modern medicine caught up with the dreaded disease and sanatoriums of this nature were no longer needed. The program was discontinued at Seaside in 1958, the patients transferred to Uncas on Thames Hospital. Since the documentary record is no longer available, it is unknown how many children died at Seaside during this time. Even under the best conditions, however, mortality rates of persons afflicted with tuberculosis prior to WWII were particularly high, many of whom could

Known as the Seaside Sanatorium, and later as Seaside Regional
Center, in the town of Waterford. An abandoned hospital where
electronic voice phenomena (EVP) is still quite active.

Seaside Sanatorium as viewed from the sea.

expect to be dead within five years of diagnosis. The disease was considerably more deadly to children and the elderly. For a compound of Seaside's size, which probably contained about 300 beds and was full to capacity throughout its history as a tuberculosis sanatorium, we can assume that quite a lot of children succumbed during their stay.

In 1959, the place was reopened as Seaside Geriatric Hospital and was administratively transferred to the Department of Health, Office of Tuberculosis Control, Hospital Care and Rehabilitation. It may also have been administered by the Welfare Department in its first year. By February of 1961, however, admissions of this nature to the Hospital were stopped and administration again changed hands.

In May of 1961, the place became Seaside Regional Center for the Mentally Retarded. Originally under the administration of the Department of Health, Office of Mental Retardation, reorganization in 1975 placed it under the Department of Mental Retardation (DMR).

The *Hartford Courant* covered an official inquiry that took place in 1972 of the Seaside facility, particularly charges of abuse and mismanagement of funds. Seaside's superintendent at that time was one Fred F. Finn, upon whom much of the blame was placed. At least eleven current and former employees came forward with statements asserting that Finn had personally beaten and abused patients at the Center. Also implicated were Mr. and Mrs. Tracy, retired employees and relatives of Finn. Senator Peter Cashman called publicly for Finn's immediate dismissal. Numerous officials from the State Health and State Personnel Commission became involved, as well as lawyers on both sides. Allegations were investigated by private investigators into the charges of abuse, and professional accountants into charges of financial mismanagement.[3]

Among the most disturbing of the abuse charges was an incident in 1969, when Finn reportedly had dragged and thrown a retarded girl down the stairs, the girl suffering a cut lip, reddened and swollen face, and a leg bruise. Employees told the board of inquiry that they had not reported the incident at the time out of fear of Finn and his colleagues. Other incidents included Finn allegedly having fired a revolver in the unit, and the Tracys shouting and swearing at the children, as well as using the inmates to buy expensive gifts for the Finns. The Tracys were accused of selling old Tracy family clothing at inflated prices to the patients, kicking patients, getting drunk, and of once throwing a soda can at a patient.[4]

Finn was further accused of having once pulled the hair of a male patient so hard that a handful of hair came out. One former employee allegedly witnessed two other incidents of abuse by Finn. The employee had been a thirteen-year-old volunteer at the facility at the time of the first incident (ten years prior to his testimony). The first of these incidents was recalled as having occurred in the early 1960s, though the employee was unsure of the exact year. He remembered that on one occasion two young boys were taken by Finn down into the boiler room and returned beaten up. He described one as having a bloody nose and the other as having a broken tooth. Both had "torn and tattered clothing," perhaps implying a sexual assault. The other incident, supposed to have occurred one Christmas night in 1966 or 1967, involved Finn having beaten and slapped the head of a patient, and that during the beating, Finn broke his watch, became enraged and beat the patient more severely. The employee stated that he had been too terrified of Finn at the time to have said anything. This former employee's testimony was regarded as suspect by Finn's lawyers, since the employee himself had been reported for allegedly striking a patient in July of 1969.[5]

Other employees in better standing at the facility charged incidents of physical and verbal abuse by Finn, too numerous to list here. Several respected professionals came to Finn's defense and refuted the testimony of others. The lengthy inquiry lasted through much of July and concluded in August of 1972. Whatever the truth of the matter, Finn was cleared of any wrongdoing. He was replaced six years later.[6]

By 1985, Seaside had become one of the largest facilities of its kind. It served about 200 residents and 700 nonresidents of 29 towns.[7]

After the events of 1972, however, it appeared to some that no one looked too closely at patient care or insisted upon disclosure of patient records, including patient deaths... at least not until the 1990s. During its three separate incarnations, Seaside dealt with hundreds, if not thousands, of patients. These patients belonged to very fragile elements of the population, among whom death is very common; first, diseased children, then the elderly, and finally, the mentally retarded. These patient groups also represented elements that were largely unwanted or given up on by society at large. Nobody noticed that those in charge, particularly the DMR, answered to almost no one, including the families of patients.

When reports of unnecessary deaths of mentally retarded patients, due to abuse or neglect by healthcare workers, began to surface in the 1990s, parents who demanded to know the circumstances of their loved ones' deaths were stonewalled by the DMR executives. Vague assurances of internal investigations were made, the results of which were never made public, even to the families of patients who had died. When parents demanded formal autopsies by forensic specialists, bodies were shuffled off as cadavers to medical students, dissected and ruined for any criminal forensics examination. Such was the case with young Lisa Barry.

Lisa Barry was a twenty-one-year-old girl who suffered from cerebral palsy, due to an umbilical cord having been wrapped around her neck during birth. Her parents, Michael and Kathy Barry, cared for her as best they could as her condition worsened over the years. They began leaving her at Seaside for brief stays, usually for no more than a few days. On Lisa's eighth stay, toward the end of 1997, she died of a seizure. She had been taking Depakote tablets to prevent these seizures.

Lisa's father, Michael Barry, became suspicious when her room was cleaned out and he heard pills rattling in her medication bottles. When he checked them, he found eight pills remained. Had Lisa been taking her medicine, as healthcare workers were responsible for ensuring, there would only have been two pills left. The Barrys demanded answers from Seaside and from the DMR. They requested an autopsy to determine if Lisa's death had been caused by negligence.

Instead, the DMR assured them that it would conduct its own internal inquiry, called a mortality review. The parents would afterward find out, however, that the results of these reviews are never disclosed to the public unless the DMR is forced to do so via a court order. In addition, Lisa's body was sent to Dr. Jack Hasson, a man with no training in criminal forensics, and his pathology class at the University of Connecticut in order to determine a cause of death. Dr. Hasson was never told to do a blood test on Lisa's body, which would have determined the level of Depakote in her system. Dr. Hasson had simply assumed that the cadaver had been sent to him, like so many other cadavers from various institutions, for training and educational purposes. The requisite amount of blood for proper testing was never drawn from Lisa.

Legal action against the DMR followed, filed by Old Lyme attorney Michael Quinn, on behalf of the Barrys. Lisa's story, and several others of mentally retarded patients who had reportedly died due to errors or negligence, was taken up by the *Hartford Courant*. *Courant* investigators Dave Altimari and Elizabeth Hamilton eventually published their disturbing findings in a two-part expose entitled "Fatal Errors, Secret Deaths," in December of 2001. The Barrys settled their lawsuit against the DMR for $750,000 and moved out of state. When asked why, by an interviewer, Michael Barry said, "The state killed my daughter, then they wouldn't take responsibility for it or tell us how it happened."[8]

By then, however, Seaside had closed its doors, seemingly forever. The facility closed in 1996, its patients transferred to state-owned properties in local communities. Just a year before its closing, the beautiful U-shaped Tudor building overlooking Long Island Sound had been added to the National Registry of Historic Places (Building #95001007). Its elegant gables now overhang windows that have been shattered by stones thrown by young vandals, its rich walls have gaping holes ripped into them, through which prospective looters and thrill seekers have entered. It sits abandoned and seemingly forgotten.

After the facility's closure, state and local officials debated for eighteen months on what to do with it. It was offered to the town, but refused as it would be too expensive to restore and maintain. A developer named Mark S. Steiner of Farmington was designated in 2000 as the preferred developer. Steiner wanted to create age-restricted housing. He offered $2.5 million and agreed that the historic buildings of the thirty-six-acre compound would be renovated and that public access to the shoreline be retained. After the legal wrangling of zoning regulations were resolved, it appeared the project would go through and Seaside would be restored to its former glory. But then, the contracting scandals involving Governor Rowland were made public, the public works commissioner fired, and the project was shelved. Now, the new Commissioner James Fleming believes the property to be valued at $7 million to $9 million, and negotiations of price and procedure have been bogged down for the past ten years.[9]

What is Seaside's future? That mystery may be as difficult to penetrate as its past...

Our Investigation

Due to the intriguing history of this abandoned place, I felt Seaside would be well worth a paranormal investigation. I pitched the idea to Matt Sinsigalli, founder of the New England Paranormal Video Research Group (NEPVRG) and he agreed. We began to make plans to assemble a team and see what sort of evidence we could capture.

I first traveled to the abandoned Seaside facility in Waterford one early morning in January 2007. I was alone, and brought only a Kodak digital camera for photographs. I wanted to scout out the facility to decide whether it warranted a full investigation. Parking in the overgrown, abandoned parking lot by an abandoned garage, I proceeded through the metal gate that said "Pedestrians Welcome." I passed the architecturally impressive old Superintendent's building, originally designed by architect Fred Langdon of New London and completed in 1934 at a cost of $28,000. The Normandy-style duplex with its many distinctive gabled windows had been much expanded since then, and probably housed several more employees before its final closure and abandonment. It now sits forlorn and forgotten, its doors boarded and many of its windows shattered.

A short walk beyond, I found the Seaside Regional Center proper, along a beautiful stretch of beach overlooking the Sound. The place was impressive with its center spire and rounded brick towers. I circled the facility taking many more photos and discovered a playground on the shore side. The rusted swing sets and other playground apparatus still stand in various stages of neglect and decay. The entire grounds are overgrown, some with foliage growing right into the ground level windows. Most of these windows and doors are boarded.

After thoroughly photographing the outside of the sprawling horseshoe-shaped complex, I proceeded within through one of the open doors. I was amazed at the degree of damage and deterioration that had taken place in just a decade, since the facility closed its doors in 1996. Peeling vinyl paint gave every wall a jagged appearance, as well as littering the floor with debris that made my every footstep crunch audibly as I walked along. In many places, parts of the ceiling had collapsed and floor tiles had come loose. Even during the day, the interior was pitch dark. As I had not thought to bring a flashlight, I had to proceed with extreme caution.

Seaside Sanatorium, first floor interior doorway.

Seaside Sanatorium, first floor neglected cabinets.

Seaside Sanatorium, first floor corridor.

Seaside Sanatorium, first floor, ceiling partially collapsed.

Seaside Sanatorium, first floor freezer area that may have served as a morgue back when the building served as a tuberculosis hospital for children.

Seaside Sanatorium, an orb picture captured in one of the first floor freezer cells.

Seaside Sanatorium, first floor freezer area.

Seaside Sanitorium, another view of the first floor freezer area.

I successfully explored much of the first and second floors, though I had not enough time to go up to the third, the attic, or down to the basement. I photographed much of the classrooms, playrooms, dental office, kitchen, and cafeteria of the first floor, as well as a spooky corridor leading to enormous freezers (which may possibly have served as a morgue in the building's time as a tuberculosis hospital). This area was the only part of the complex that gave me a moment's twinge of uneasiness. It was in this freezer/morgue area that I captured my best and only paranormal photo of the day, out of approximately 300 photos taken. In the second freezer cell, with it's heavy wooden door leaning awkwardly off its hinges, I captured an interesting orb inside the cell, right above an abandoned chair. Nothing reflective was within, and no other cause for the light anomaly could be found.

Just like electronic voice phenomena, genuine orb pictures are extremely rare to capture. Many beginning investigators are misled by fuzzy "dust orbs" and naturally occurring reflections. I have learned that genuine orbs, of which I have captured only a half dozen out of several hundred photographs, on over a dozen different investigations, are much rarer than these commonly occurring phenomena. Still, orbs are a matter of considerable debate among investigators and difficult to classify as definitively paranormal.

The second floor is mainly administrative offices, though one large office appeared to be that of the Superintendent. This room seemed to me to have a heavy, oppressive atmosphere. But, not being a Sensitive myself, I did not give the sensation much thought as I generally defer such impressions to those much more experienced in these matters. I left the vast Seaside facility vowing to return soon. I was certain that the place warranted a thorough investigation by our team.

Unfortunately, I would not have occasion to return to Seaside for another six months. During that time, our little team of investigators had our first residential investigation

Seaside Sanatorium, second floor superintendent's office where mentally retarded patients where reportedly beaten and abused.

as well as further investigations of historic properties for the Milford Historical Society, which in turn generated more media attention than we had anticipated. Matt and I split our time between public relations, interviewing new members, media relations and interviews, and scheduled investigations, when not attending to family matters and our full-time jobs. Finally, in June our schedules freed up somewhat, and we could consider a return trip to Seaside. We decided on a Thursday evening.

On a June evening in 2007, we arrived at the neglected parking lot of the old Seaside facility. Our team consisted of me, Matt, Seth, and guest investigator Jennifer. In the absence of our regular Sensitive, who had religious commitments that prevented her from coming, Jenn brought unique skills to the investigation. In addition to being a Reiki Master and spiritual healer, she is also an Energy Sensitive who can sense lingering energies and emotions in abandoned places. Since she had also expressed an interest in spiritography, I loaned her my Infrared-converted Nikon Coolpix 5400, with external IR light for taking good digital images in darkness. For myself, I brought only my Sony Cyber-shot DSC-F717, with Nightshot capability, and my Olympus audio recorder. Matt brought an electronic voice recorder (EVR) of his own, as well as a Sony handycam with Nightshot.

We proceeded inside the Sanatorium. Matt led the way with a flashlight and handheld electromagnetic field meter (EMF), while Seth followed videotaping with the handycam. Jenn and I photographed, and from time to time I stopped to try for electronic voice phenomena (EVPs) on my EVR, through careful questioning. We explored first the classrooms and dining facilities of the first floor, then the basement and second floor offices. Two of our members had personal experiences during this time.

Seth, who does not normally credit feelings of unease or the like, said he had an unearthly chill while walking down the stairway into the basement. I later told him about the allegations of abuse, that Superintendent Finn had supposedly led boys into the basement's boiler room for physical punishments.

Jenn sensed energies of extreme negative emotions in the Superintendent's office on the second floor. She described feelings of profound sadness and fear.

Hoping for some hard data to help substantiate these personal experiences, I did a brief *Question and Answer* session in the office for EVPs. During this time, Seth reported that he had seen something move rapidly in front of me while I asked questions, which he videotaped. Upon later review of the evidence, however, this glowing object turned out to be a bug of some kind. I could just make out the flickering insect wings on the glowing light that shot in front of me.

The third floor was mostly old bedrooms (no beds remain) and bathroom facilities. The most "difficult" of the retarded patients commonly were housed on this floor. Matt and I discovered a covered walkway or corridor that led from the third floor into one of the round towers with the lighthouse-

Seaside Sanatorium basement, where at least one reported incident of violent abuse may have occurred.

like windows. I was excited to see this, since it seemed that all other entrances to the towers had been boarded up. We proceeded in and while I began to photograph up into the windowed belfry, we startled a number of nesting pigeons. The sudden racket of so many fluttering wings startled me for a moment, giving Matt a good laugh at my expense. The attic, too, had sectioned areas that may have served as bedrooms or storage. The corridor was littered with heaps of old medical records from patients that had stayed at the Center. I was surprised to see that these had not been more properly disposed of.

With the hour growing late, and Jenn and Seth having work the next morning, we said our farewells to the Seaside Sanatorium. Though not the creepiest location we had investigated, we all agreed that it was one of the most beautiful, positioned as it was by the seashore. Later review of the evidence gleaned at least two very good EVPs. One, captured by Matt during the first couple minutes after we had entered the building, was the distinct voice of a little girl, which seems to be saying "No, you're sick, you're sick!" The other, captured by me, happened after Matt dropped a piece of his equipment and muttered, "son of a bitch," while in the kitchen area. Thirty seconds later, an eerie stilted voice repeated his words, "son... of... a... bitch." It sounds like that of a young or mentally handicapped person.

All of us agreed that our personal experiences and the fun of exploration made the investigation well worth the long drive to Waterford.

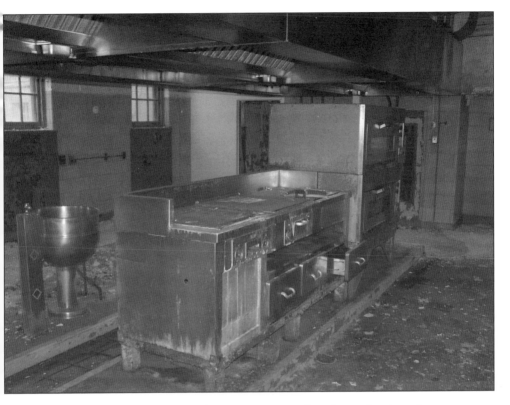

Seaside Sanatorium, first floor kitchen, and perhaps the site of an intelligent haunting? One very good EVP was captured here.

Chapter 9
Haunted Battlefield

Fort Griswold, in Groton, site of the Battle of Groton Heights, where more than eighty Americans were massacred by British troops.

Groton has the dubious honor of being Connecticut's bloodiest town. The two goriest massacres in the state's history were committed within a few miles of each other; the first committed by the colonists upon Native Americans, the other inflicted upon the colonists more than a century later by the British. It is as if the region itself is cursed with a legacy of violence. Yet Groton residents are proud of their military tradition, as evidenced by monuments, battlefield parks, and memorials, and carried on even today by the nearby Coast Guard Academy and Naval Submarine Base in its sister city of New London.

Groton's bloody legacy began with the earliest years of the Connecticut colony's settlement, and the genocide that followed. Before Puritan settlers from Massachusetts came to the Connecticut River Valley and shoreline in the early Seventeenth Century, most of southern Connecticut belonged to the powerful Native American tribe of Pequots. The River Valley tribes, fearing the warlike Pequots, invited the English to come and settle, in the hope that they might keep the Pequots at bay. An inevitable and violent clash followed, in which horrific atrocities were committed by Englishman and Pequot alike. The Pequot War of 1637 saw several skirmishes, raids, and battles, culminating in the Great Swamp Fight in what would become Fairfield, but the greatest and most decisive encounter of all was at a Pequot stronghold known as Fort Mystic. Historians have different viewpoints, some referring to the lurid events of Friday 26 May 1637, as the "Battle of Fort Mystic," others as the "Mystic Massacre." Be it battle or massacre, however, all agree it was an unequivocal victory for the Puritans which forever broke the back of Pequot power in the region.

The 110 English that comprised the expedition, armored in breastplates and helmets and armed with matchlock muskets, were led by Captains Underhill and Mason. Escorted by their Narragansett and Mohegan allies to the Pequot fort, the Puritan militia sneak attacked the palisade fort before an alarm could be raised. Wigwams were set afire during the fighting and the Puritans withdrew to surround the fort. As the community within the round palisade became a raging inferno, Pequots fleeing the flames were mercilessly and methodically shot down by musket balls. Those who never made it out of the fort were burned alive, screaming. Of the several hundred Pequots (numbers are hotly debated among historians, anywhere from 300 to 700) within the fort, only seven survived to seek shelter as slaves among the Puritan's Mohegan or Narragansett allies while another seven escaped altogether. English losses were only two killed in the fighting and twenty wounded (which has led some researchers to conclude that the fort was primarily composed of noncombatant woman and children, the men believed to have been out hunting at the time). The place has ever after been known as Pequot Hill.

Mason later wrote of the experience, "Thus did the Lord judge among the heathen, filling the place with dead bodies!" The Reverend Increase Mather, upon learning of the massacre, exhorted his faithful to "thank God that on this day we have sent 600 heathen souls to Hell!"[1]

Now, fast forward 144 years to 6 September 1781. Colonists now consider themselves Yankees, not Puritans, and are ready to assert their independence from what they consider a tyrannical Great Britain. The colonies are in full rebellion, and the British have decided to crush the coastal fort that the Groton colonists erected to protect their port town. Under the leadership of the traitor Benedict Arnold, the British forces first burn the city of New London. Arnold then orders a subordinate, Lieutenant Colonel Eyre, to take his 800 trained British soldiers and assault the fort on the Groton bank.

Fort Griswold, spot where Colonel William Ledyard was stabbed to death by his own sword, after surrendering it to a British officer.

Colonel Ledyard commands the 150 American defenders in what he must know to be a hopeless battle. The fort is taken within forty minutes of heated fighting. What follows next is a matter of considerable controversy between British and American historians.

According to American eyewitness accounts at the time, Ledyard then surrendered the fort and its surviving American defenders (these accounts contend that only about ten Americans were killed in the actual fighting). He offered his sword to Captain Bloomfield, a British officer, as a ritual token of honorable surrender. Colonel Ledyard was then repaid for his trouble by being stabbed to death with his own sword by Captain Bloomfield. Indiscriminate firing then took place by the British troops upon the Americans, all of whom had already lain down their weapons. Another British officer attempted to stop the massacre and ordered a cease fire, too late for most of the defenders. His command, though followed, was not popular among the troops, who then loaded the few wounded survivors into a wagon, rolled

Sword of Colonel William Ledyard, with which he was stabbed to death after surrendering the fort.

it to the top of a nearby hill, then released to send it crashing down into a copse of apple trees. One American who survived even the crash of the wagon and tried to crawl away had his skull crushed in with the butt of a British musket. Healthier survivors were taken prisoner, to die at sea in the notorious disease-ridden prison ships, or to later be released. At least eighty-five Americans were killed on the spot, or were mortally wounded and died shortly afterward. Some wounded who survived were taken by locals to the nearby Ebenezer Avery house to be treated.[2]

British losses were recorded to have been 51 killed in the assault and 142 wounded. Even after the battle and the massacre that followed, the British showed little mercy to the corpses of American dead (and precious little concern for their own). According to one account, "The killed of the enemy were buried by their comrades at the gate of the fort, and were so slightly covered that many of their legs and arms remained above ground; our people who were killed at the fort, were stripped, and so disfigured, covered with blood and dust, that with the exception of two or three, they could not be recognized by their friends..."[3]

Today, Fort Griswold and the Groton Monument, a granite obelisk 135 feet high, mark the site on Mount Ledyard. On the south side of the pedestal is inscribed a list of eighty-five names, of the Americans who fell at the fort on 6 September. Inside the adjacent museum, you can still see the sword of Colonel Ledyard, encased in glass. But the story does not end there...[4]

So much trauma and death, despite a paucity of supernatural lore, seemed a good indicator of a possible paranormal hotspot. At least one other paranormal investigation of Fort Griswold had taken place, in July of 2005 (the article can be found at the Haunted Times website) by members of the New England Paranormal Research Agency and the Atlantic Coast Paranormal Research Group. They claim to have retrieved sporadic pieces of evidence such as

Ebenezer Avery House, historic property opened seasonally to the public. Many of the wounded from the battle at Fort Griswold were taken here.

Fort Griswold, obelisk and Monument House Museum, where one can view the sword of Colonel Ledyard among other artifacts, and learn the history of Connecticut's most famous battle.

photos and EVPs. A member of Connecticut Paranormal, a separate group, told me in personal conversation that his team obtained some very good EVPs from the Covered Way, in which a ghostly voice spoke in an English accent. Are the battlefields of Fort Griswold and Fort Mystic truly haunted? Our team could barely wait to find out...

Our Investigation

I first drove out to Fort Griswold on the afternoon of Wednesday 17 September 2006, to get some good daytime photos of area. I knew the group would be coming out for a night investigation the following evening, but I also knew that good photos of the monument, museum, and other buildings would be difficult at night. I also hoped to pinpoint the location of the Fort Mystic massacre, which I knew to have occurred on what is now Pequot Hill.

I spent a very scenic and peaceful time photographing the impressive monument (a giant obelisk reaching up to the sky) and the nearby museum. I then moved on to Fort Griswold proper and snapped pics of the ruined hill-like fortifications, the gate and its placard listing the dead and fallen of the battle, stones marking the death sites of the American Colonel Ledyard and British officer William Montgomery (both with inscribed placards commemorating the site), the Ebenezer Avery House (where the wounded were taken after the battle), the historic Powder Magazine building, and the Shot Furnace. The impressive stone entrance gate, with its cannon and bronze plaque listing the American dead, wounded and escaped, stands directly across from the street sign marking the intersection of Park Avenue and Monument Street. My only companions were a few artists painting scenes of the New London and Groton harbor on their easels and some wandering tourists.

Though I acquired many good photos, none were remotely paranormal, nor did I get any strange or eerie feelings about the place. It just felt very peaceful, as if the

Statue of Captain John Mason, leader of the Connecticut colonists in the Massacre of Fort Mystic, killing over 600 Pequots. The statue originally stood upon the site of the killings, on Groton's Pequot Avenue, but has since been relocated at the request of modern Pequots to Windsor's Palisado Avenue.

hundred and thirty or so British and American dead had long since reconciled themselves to rest.

My drive to nearby Pequot Avenue, on Pequot Hill, proved fruitless. The place was entirely residential, without a single historic stature, placard, or monument of any kind to commemorate the bloody massacre that had occurred beneath the quiet suburban homes. Absolutely nothing of public land to investigate remained. In speaking with one local, I learned that a statue of Captain John Mason (leader of the colonists in the massacre of Native Americans) had existed at the junction of what is now the intersection of Clift Street and Pequot Avenue. The statue has since been removed, at the request of modern Pequots (it has been relocated to Palisado Avenue in Windsor, Connecticut), and only a Monkey Tree plant remains to mark the spot. I asked a friendly local who had lived on the hill more than thirty years if she had every witnessed any unusual phenomena on the street. She laughed good-humoredly, "No, no, nothing like that."

Fort Griswold, boulder with plaque indicating the spot where British Major William Montgomery was killed in the fighting.

Fort Griswold interior, showing the Covered Way and locked storehouse.

Matt and I returned to Fort Griswold on the evening of Thursday 18 September 2006. Gail was unable to join us due to a sudden illness, and Seth and Haydon had work commitments that prevented them coming. Instead, we took our newest investigator-in-training, Trisha.

We brought with us two Sony camcorders with night-shot, an EMF meter, and two digital voice recorders. I also brought my cheap digital camera for still photos, though I was not too hopeful of any quality pics, given the openness of the terrain and the limited flash of my camera. Even if we found no paranormal evidence, Matt and I figured the expedition would be a good training experience for Trisha.

We walked throughout the interior and exterior of the fort. One video camera Matt set up looking upon Colonel Ledyard's death site, the other Trisha and I took to roam about and see what we could capture. We got footage of all the sites worth seeing, including the tunnel known as the Covered Way leading from the interior to the exterior of the fort. Strong winds and the presence of a small group of teenagers that came to wander about briefly complicated the investigation. Added to this, the open layout of the site proved difficult to cover with just three people.

Trisha also roved the interior of the fort, where the massacre proper had occurred, asking questions of the dead while holding the voice recorder and EMF meter. Neither of us observed any unusual EMF readings or spikes. In fact, the needle remained at one or below the entire time. Trisha thought she captured her first EVP at one point when she asked of any entities present, "Are you at peace?" and thought she recorded a voice that said, "yes." Upon later analysis, this proved to be merely wind.

Hours later, just before Matt and I decided to pack it in and call it a night, we laid upon the battlement facing the harbor. I continued to ask questions, allowing thirty seconds or so between, into my recorder. Later analysis would show this to be the time of our only captured evidence from the

Fort Griswold, view of the sea from battlements. It was near here that the author captured his very first EVP.

investigation. While looking down upon the field where the British would have marched upon the fort's defenders, I asked "Did any of you know that you would die that day?"

An EVP was recorded almost immediately afterward. It distinctly sounds like a male voice, in a whisper and at a very low hertz range that a human voice could not have made. At the time, we three were the only people left in the park. What is being said, however, would later be debated by every member of the team who listened to it. It sounds like an answer to my question, possibly the word "probably" or maybe even "from the sea." It is a Class "C" EVP at best, and the only evidence of anything paranormal gathered that night.

As far as personal experiences, none of us reported having felt any uneasiness at any time. In fact, we all agreed the place, even at night, was one of serenity and peace. It is certainly worth visiting, but be respectful of those who died there and of the history of the place. The history alone is worth the trip.

Chapter 10
Norwich Insane Asylum

Norwich Asylum, Administration Building.

Recent archaeological evidence from digs at the site of the abandoned Norwich State Hospital indicate that it was the site of a Native American village about 5,000 years ago. According to State Archaeologist Nicholas Bellantoni, about 8,800 artifacts have been uncovered so far, which suggest a "unique village setting for the time."[1]

The original asylum, dubbed the Norwich State Hospital for the Insane, was established in 1904. The site comprised a pair of two-story buildings, one for women and one, known as Salmon Hall, for male patients. A cottage on the grounds was erected for doctors. Forty patients transferred from Middletown brought the total number of patients up to fifty-one, with space enough to accommodate 104. A tuberculosis sanatorium established in 1912 added another administrative building and two shacks for patients. The insane asylum and tuberculosis hospital would quickly fill to capacity, eventually join as one institution, and be forced to expand their facilities throughout the twentieth century. The site eventually encompassed several buildings spread out over 470 acres, many connected via underground tunnels.[2]

The first documented tragedy to occur at the asylum was the suicide of a patient. Edward K. Arvine, a lawyer, had voluntarily admitted himself as a sufferer of "melancholia." In December of 1914, he hanged himself in his room with an improvised rope of torn bedclothes, attached to an iron grating. His death would be but the first of many tragedies at the institution.[3] An explosion of a hot water heater in 1919 killed two employees, teamster Fred Ladd and night attendant Thomas Duggan.[4] Hospital cook Fred Smith, while crossing the road, was struck and killed in 1925, by an automobile driven by Robert Anderson, a supervisor at the nearby tuberculosis sanatorium.[5] Annie Prudenthal, a trained nurse and former patient at the hospital, killed herself with a knife at her home in 1930, after having been discharged from the Norwich Hospital only a few days before.[6]

In December of 1934, Sheriff Michael Carroll attempted to serve papers committing one Leonard Gosselin to Norwich Hospital. Rather than allow himself to be committed to the infamous asylum, Gosselin killed Sheriff Carroll with a shotgun blast, then turned the gun on himself. Gosselin was found dead in his apartment by Patrolman Clifford Crary.[7]

In December of 1941, the State Public Welfare Council began an investigation into the suspicious death of Norwich patient William Smith. Smith had a chronic heart ailment and had been mistakenly administered sedatives by an attendant, causing a fatal overdose.[8]

The name of the asylum was shortened to the Norwich State Hospital in 1926, and until 1971 the Hospital housed

Norwich Asylum's Salmon Hall.

and treated the very worst criminally insane patients that Connecticut had to offer. The majority of murderers, rapists, and violent criminals that successfully copped an insanity plea found themselves committed to the infamous Salmon Hall, the asylum's maximum-security building. The rogues' list of patient inmates that passed through its doors is a long one...

September of 1918, patient Solomon Brooks escaped the asylum, found his way home and killed his wife Rachael with a bread knife.[9] Ernest Skinner, a seventeen-year-old murderer who had hacked to death his neighbor with a hatchet and set him on fire, was admitted in 1922.[10] In 1928, twenty-one-year-old mother Mrs. Emma Muscarella, who confessed to the choking death of her one-day-old son, was admitted.[11] In 1938, after having been convicted of shooting and killing a New Haven deputy sheriff in a 1936 holdup, murderer John Palm was spared the electric chair after pleading insanity and transferred to the Norwich asylum.[12] Mrs. Florence Schwartz was committed in 1938 after asphyxiating and killing her eleven-year-old daughter.[13]

An investigation of Norwich State Hospital by the State's Attorney and the Governor in 1944 followed a massive manhunt by State Police for two escaped patients. Both Carl Wilson and Edward Dzeidzic were violently insane, and experienced escapees. It was Wilson's third escape from the institution and Dzeidzic's fourth. Wilson had previously served five years in the state prison for manslaughter after killing a man at a card game in 1924. In 1936, he slashed a man with a knife, and in 1941, he was arrested after shooting a Hartford youth in the leg. Dzeidzic had been arrested after firing a shotgun at a group of children. Though the Norwich asylum had enforced progressively more severe restrictions on Wilson and Dzeidzic, it appeared that the hospital just could not hold them. The two were eventually recaptured.[14]

Charles Beausoleil confessed to stabbing his elderly parents to death in 1952 and was ordered permanently confined to Norwich State Hospital, after a judge's decision found him to be insane.[15]

The testimony of one Albert Taborsky against his brother, Joseph Taborsky, in the shooting death of a package store owner four years previously, was called into question in 1954 following Albert's committal to Norwich State Hospital. Joseph Taborsky's lawyers cited Albert's insanity as cause for doubting his eyewitness account of the crime, in an attempt to keep Joseph from the electric chair. The media billed the trial as the infamous "Cain and Abel" Case.[16]

Leroy Reddick, the so-called "dynamite killer," was sentenced to life imprisonment at the Norwich State Hospital in 1954. He had exploded the truck of one Homer Wright in New Haven in 1952, killing both Wright and his wife, Ophelia.[17]

Everett Cooley, the "Lovers Lane Slayer," after an imprisonment at Norwich for the killing of twenty-two-year-old John Davis and the attack upon his nineteen-year-old fiancé, was declared by hospital psychiatrists to be sane enough to stand trial for his crimes in 1957. His brother and accessory, Milton Cooley, was already serving a life sentence at Wethersfield State Prison. The pair had also been convicted of the kidnapping of a North Branford housewife and an attack upon her husband.[18]

Mrs. Joan Gronwoldt of Granby, after being tried for manslaughter for shooting and killing her two children, was declared legally insane in 1961 and remanded to the Norwich institution. A diagnosed schizophrenic, she had frequent hallucinations and delusions of an "approaching black hand and a knife being thrust slowly into her heart." She also believed in a childhood memory of her hometown being invaded by rats, and of having watched them being shot down by the thousands.[19]

Even after the closing of Norwich's maximum-security Salmon Hall in 1971, more of Connecticut's worst criminally insane continued to end up at the institution. Among these were Garcia Reyes, who stabbed to death three children in 1967, after his romantic advances toward their mother were rebuffed. He reportedly heard voices he believed to be from the devil that told him to commit violent acts.[20]

Another justified his violence as the work of God. Twenty-two-year-old Matthew Naab claimed that he had stabbed his grandmother, Anna Naab, to death in 1974 because she was "possessed of the devil." He was committed to Norwich Hospital, where he was declared "psychotic and insane," and the murder an "acute episode of schizophrenia."[21]

Even more embarrassing for the Norwich Hospital than the numerous escapes of patients over the years, were the instances of violently insane patients being prematurely released. Such was the case of twenty-three-year-old Gregory Gillespie. After the shooting of a Hartford man, Wade Foote, in 1974, in an incident of road rage following a motor vehicle accident, Gillespie was acquitted of first degree assault on grounds of insanity. Foote had been unarmed and was shot five times by Gillespie, wounds from which he eventually recovered. By June of 1975, Norwich psychiatrists declared that Gillespie was no longer a threat to himself or others, and he was granted leave. Then, in May of 1976, a lovers' quarrel with sixteen-year-old Shereese Weatherly resulted in Gillespie shooting her four times with a handgun in front of her home, killing Weatherly. Gillespie surrendered to police the same day.[22]

During that same summer of 1975, another man was admitted to Norwich Hospital after stabbing a Hartford man (who later recovered) during one of his schizophrenic fits. Twenty-four-year-old John Franklin was sent to Norwich Hospital in April, but by July was declared sane and safe enough to be released. In March of 1976, just eight months after his release, Franklin broke into the home of neighbors Leonard and Madaline Flannery. Madaline witnessed Franklin stab her husband twenty-one times, killing him as she fled out the front door to a neighbor's house. Franklin was afterward committed to Norwich Hospital indefinitely.[23]

Up until 1981, defendants in state courts entered pleas of not guilty by reason of insanity, but in 1981, a new law allowed for pleas of guilty to be followed by findings of insanity. Such was the case with twenty-three-year-old William Johnston, who had shot gunned his father and mother in November of 1981. His father, Murray Johnston, was killed though the mother, Barbara Keyes, survived. Johnston entered a plea of guilty, but was still found to be mentally incompetent by a three-judge panel and sent to Norwich State Hospital. He was declared a paranoid schizophrenic who heard voices telling him to shoot his father.[24]

A similar incident occurred with former Norwich patient Thomas Auduskevicz. A three-panel judge in 1984 found him "guilty but not criminally responsible" in the strangulation death of his mother, Barbara Auduskevicz. Auduskevicz was another paranoid schizophrenic obsessed with voices. Barbara Auduskevicz was found dead in her garage in December of 1982, the cause of death having been strangulation, though she also suffered deep knife wounds to both sides of her neck.[25]

The Hospital complex became a microcosm society, especially for the criminally insane and the staff expected to treat them. The bedlam created at many times became a powder keg of violence when staff members who had been assaulted visited reprisals on particularly troublesome inmates. Added to this intentional mistreatment are early primitive methods, begun with the best of intentions, but no less inhumane for that. Early doctors believed in mechanical restraint, sometimes for days at a time, as a legitimate form of treatment for mental illness. Hydrotherapy was also used, as suspension in water was believed to have therapeutic effects.

As early as 1921, a point was raised to the Hospital Appropriations Committee, and seriously considered, that the "hopelessly insane" be put to death. The suggestion was considered after committeemen were shown a madman who had been shackled to his bed for five years.[26]

Conditions at the Hospital, and allegations of abuse, were investigated several times. Governor Baldwin ordered a full investigation in 1939. The investigative team found

Norwich Asylum, hydrotherapy tank where patients were immersed in icy water.

that condition of care was below the necessary standard, for a number of reasons relating to personnel and supplies, but could find no evidence to confirm abuse.[27]

A former inmate of Norwich State Hospital, however, spoke out in a May 1946 editorial in the *Hartford Courant*. The editorial gives firsthand eyewitness testimony of patients being starved, beaten, and packed in ice for hours as a form of punishment.[28]

In April of 1967, three hospital guards were attacked by patients in Norwich's Salmon building where the very worst of the criminally insane were confined. State police investigated the incident, in which patients had set a fire in an apparent escape attempt.[29] In 1982, hospital staff protested work shortages and assaults by violent patients. Union workers picketed and cited examples to the media of workers having been kicked, hit, and bitten. They also demanded clearer definitions by administration of patient restraint versus patient abuse, since employees had been disciplined for having to forcibly restrain violent patients.

One psychiatric aide said that he had "suffered blackened eyes, broken ribs, chairs smashed over his head and other assaults." He also stated that he had been "threatened with knives" and "broken his teeth."[30]

By far, the most infamous building at Norwich was the hospital's Salmon Hall. One of the first two buildings of the complex, it originally served as housing for male patients. By 1930, as many more buildings were added to the growing complex, Salmon was renovated to serve as a maximum-security building. Windows were barred and caged doors riveted in place, forming prison-like cells. After 1930, most criminally insane were transferred to the Norwich facility. Until its shut down in 1971, Salmon generally held around 700 imprisoned criminally insane, though at times it held considerably more.[31]

In October of 1971, this most infamous building closed its doors. The criminally insane were transferred to a much larger, newer facility at Connecticut Valley Hospital in Middletown. Media hailed the decision, describing Salmon as that "trouble-plagued maximum security center at Norwich" and as a "cramped, drab prison building at the hospital." Though inmates had been constantly locked down for the past three and a half years, in squalid prison conditions, it had not prevented escapes. As recently as August of 1971, inmate Robert M. Layne of Glastonbury escaped Salmon and the Norwich facility. He was eventually recaptured after having gunned down two policemen in Spencer, Massachusetts.[32]

Another article in the *Hartford Courant* cheered "The state is finally going to close down its disgraceful 'maximum security' unit for the criminally insane at Norwich… the ancient, inadequate and infamous Salmon Building."

Norwich continued to function as a treatment hospital until it finally closed its doors in 1996, and its remaining patients transferred to Connecticut Valley Hospital. It now stands in picturesque abandon. Security guards herd off spiritographers and thrill seekers who seek to photograph the still-impressive architecture, as well as urban explorers who seek adventure in the depths of its underground tunnels. At least one doctor who used to work at the facility claims that the tunnel beneath Salmon Hall is definitely haunted. He claims that violent inmates were chained to chairs in this tunnel, burned by cigarettes, and beaten by aides. He describes them as the failed experiments of doctors, who now haunt these tunnels and who seek revenge on anyone who ventures there.

The place is so spooky, in fact, that VH-1 decided to film its new Celebrity Paranormal show on the Norwich grounds. As part of a deal with the town, they changed the name of the place in their episode to the "Warson Hospital for the Criminally Insane." Episodes 2 and 4 were filmed at the location in 2006, with a back story of one Nell Marley, supposedly committed in 1945 for murder. Episode 2 was entitled "Pearl" after the entity which Marley supposedly claimed had possessed her during her crime. Though the story of Nell Marley and "Pearl" appears to have been completely fabricated, the show was nevertheless a huge success.[33]

Is the Norwich State Hospital truly haunted? We could hardly wait to find out!

Our Investigation

Though I had always been interested in an investigation of the Norwich Hospital, and particularly the Salmon building, everything I had read online insisted that the town had closed the place off to visitors. Security, it was said, was diligent about rounding up intruders and herding them off property or worse, having them arrested by State Police for trespassing. So, any investigation was put on the back burner until the situation changed, while we investigated other worthy sites.

Early in 2007, Matt and I began an email correspondence with another younger group of paranormal investigators, who were looking for guidance and a presentation by older, more experienced investigators. While speaking to Steve, the founder of the group, we were told that his group was intimately familiar with the Norwich facility and knew its grounds, the tunnels and, most importantly, the security personnel. We were assured that, if we were interested, he could get us in to investigate the facility provided that we were brief and respectful to security staff.

I, of course, was interested from the beginning. Though we could not gain official permission from the town of Preston (to which the majority of the property currently belongs, until the site is sold to Utopia Studios or some other developer), a brief investigation was possible through connections among the security staff, providing we were discreet.

On a Thursday evening in March 2007, Matt and I, along with our newest Investigator-in-Training Cynthia, met with three members of the Haunting Hunters; the founder Steve, Brittany, and Kevin. Armed with our camcorders, digital cameras and voice recorders, the six of us proceeded to the grounds.

We came first to the Administration Building, where VH-1 filmed much of their Celebrity Paranormal show. The

Norwich Asylum's infamous Salmon Hall building. Picture was taken at night with infrared camera.

impressive staircase, safe, and small chapel area (not to be confused with the nearby Chapel building) all made great photos. Only later, upon review of the evidence, would we discover that Steve's group got some great EVPs while in this building. One seems to say "you've got pretty bones" or "carry him home." Another voice says "I am waiting."

Unfortunately, I was too busy snapping pictures with my digital camera and juggling my Sony handycam trying to get decent video. I forgot to turn on my voice recorder until we arrived at our next destination: the Salmon building.

Salmon Hall was truly as spooky as I had imagined. The building was locked from the outside and could only be entered through the underground tunnels. Walking the dark gloomy corridor, I recalled the legends of abused patients said to haunt this tunnel. I even found wooden chairs left in the tunnels, where supposedly patients had been chained and beaten, or burned with lit cigarettes. No chains remained, however.

On the upper level, I photographed the eerie hallway while Matt followed Steven and Kevin with his handycam (Cynthia and Brittany had opted to remain in the Administration Building). Individual cells were outfitted much like prison cells, with barred windows and locked chain-link doors. They also bore an uncomfortable resemblance to animal cages. The remains of patient bed frames were found throughout, though the mattresses were long gone.

It was up here that, for a brief time, I became separated from the others. Too involved in my photographing of the cages, I had not noticed that the other three had already proceeded to the next level up. It was during this ten or fifteen minutes that my only EVPs of the night occurred. Of course, I did not realize this until much later when I was reviewing the evidence at home. While photographing the empty cells, after each flash of the camera (for about 3 seconds), a deep male voice said "smile!"

Norwich Asylum, tunnels beneath Salmon Hall, believed to be haunted by the spirits of abused patients.

Norwich Asylum, Salmon Hall, caged rooms where criminally insane inmates were kept.

I rejoined the others and investigated the rest of Salmon Hall. The upper level was much like the first. Some of the rooms appear to have been communal, with large windows looking out upon the complex. After we were done, we rejoined the women and proceeded back into the tunnels.

We came next to the Women's Building, and its impressive auditorium. We photographed and videotaped this area extensively. The enormous empty windows leered down at us, and the torn and dilapidated theater seats. I took my most interesting photograph of the night while alone on the stage.

After walking carefully up the wooden stairs onto the torn-up stage area, I snapped two photos of the left section and two of the right. My Sony Cyber-Shot DSC-F717 camera had a nifty feature called NightShot (exactly like that of the handycams), which allowed for photos in complete blackness, without a flash, via infrared illuminators. To extend the

Norwich Asylum auditorium.

range of the infrared light, Matt had loaned me his HVL-IRM infrared attachment that extends the range of the Sony NightShot. Unfortunately, photos taken with NightShot tend to be colorless and grainy, particularly around the edges. Therefore, my only unique photo is not the best quality.

The picture shows what looks to be the shadow or silhouette of a man standing side profile. The silhouette appears upon the stacked-up ladders and scaffolding materials shoved in the back of the stage. I was the only one on stage at the time, and no source of illumination (infrared or otherwise) was behind me. No object between the IR light of my camera and the scaffolding stood in the way to have cast a shadow. The silhouette clearly shows, to my eye at least, a nose and chin and a billed hat. Nobody in our group that night wore a hat with a bill.

Matt and I would examine this photo at length later on. Unfortunately, it is difficult to say definitively that it is paranormal. In order to be certain, we would have to go back and try to recreate the image. For a variety of reasons, however,

Norwich Asylum, auditorium stage, note the unexplained silhouette against the wall of what looks like a shadowy man in a billed hat.

this is nearly impossible. The best I can say, therefore, is that the image certainly is interesting and is enough to cast a "shadow" of doubt.

A last trip through the tunnels and we had to bid the Norwich Hospital goodbye. Though we did not have the time or luxury of exploring more of the buildings, we felt we had gathered some good evidence and had shared in a unique experience.

Chapter 11
Thrice Cursed Island

Charles Island, believed to be haunted by a triple curse, at low tide. The sandbar can be crossed from Silver Sands Beach in Milford at low tide, but be wary of rising water!

Milford's Charles Island has the unique reputation of an island that has been cursed three times over. Legends of Indian curses, pirate treasure, and a headless ghost have inspired thrill seekers and treasure hunters for generations. Proponents of the curse legend site as evidence the fact that none of the many mercantile ventures begun on the island ever met with success, as well as the numerous drowning deaths in and around the sandbar that connects the island with Milford's Silver Sands beach at low tide. Indians, pirates, and ghosts aside, the island has also hosted various farming enterprises, a mansion, a luxury hotel, a fish oil factory, and a religious retreat for Dominican priests and lay people, all of which met with disaster and failure.

Charles Island has such a long and colorful history, interwoven with its several legends, that it is best to begin at the beginning.

Before the arrival of English colonists to the Milford area, the island belonged to the Paugussett tribe of Native Americans, who called it Poquahaug. The island was reportedly a favorite summer resort of the Paugussetts, from which the tribe's sachem, Ansantawae, entertained guests in his "big wigwam." Ansantawae sold the island in 1639 to a company of 40 English settlers, along with a large track of mainland in what would become Milford, for the paltry cost of "6 coats, 10 blankets, 1 kettle, 12 hatchets, 12 hoes, 2 dozen knives, and a dozen small glasses."[1]

The first of Charles Island's three curses allegedly began with Ansantawae. According to the legend, the chieftain had a very beautiful daughter, admired by Indian and white man alike. Sometime after the sale of the island had been completed and before the Paugussetts moved west to join with other tribes, this beautiful Indian princess was "kidnapped," presumably by one of the colonists. The chieftain then cursed the island so that it would never benefit or profit any white man.[2]

The island then changed hands several times over the next few years, as each new owner discovered the soil inhospitable for farming. George Hubbard, a planter, first owned the land in 1640, but soon after sold it to a Richard Bryan. Bryan, in turn, sold the land in 1657 to Charles Deal, from whom the island gets its modern name. Deal tried his hand at a tobacco plantation, which failed miserably.

Upon the death of Charles Deal in 1685, the island changed hands several more times, through death and inheritance. By 1698, it ended up in the ownership of Elizabeth Couch, who lived in England and whose father had been the previous owner. It was during this time, while Elizabeth served as absentee owner, that the island acquired its most enduring legend of all.

Captain William Kidd, one of the most infamous pirates ever to sail the high seas, may have made a brief stop at Charles Island in June of 1699. Despite the price on his head, good documentary evidence exists that he visited the residents of Milford two or three times, walking openly about the town. At the time, before he proceeded to Block Island, Kidd sent a lawyer to Boston to negotiate his surrender, in return for amnesty. Such terms had been successfully negotiated by previous pirates, and so Kidd had no reason to suspect treachery by the Boston governor, Lord Bellomont.

Kidd's subsequent arrest upon his arrival at Boston harbor, deportation to England, and public execution at London's Execution Dock on 23 May 1701, are a matter of historic record. What happened prior to his arrival at Boston, however, is a subject of much debate. Kidd did, in fact, bury at least some of his treasure on Gardiner's Island, near Long Island, which was later reclaimed by British authorities. This treasure amounted to £14,000, only a fraction of the £100,000 Kidd claimed to have hidden before his death. Legend has it that Kidd placed a curse upon his buried treasures to prevent looters.

An 1838 history of the New Haven Colony claims that Kidd buried treasure on the south side of Charles Island prior to his final, fatal voyage. The legend spawned by this brief account has evolved into Charles Island's most enduring ghost legend, and the second of the three-part Curse Cycle.

According to this account, by local Nineteenth Century historian Edward Lambert, Kidd's treasure was discovered one moonlit night by two adventurous young men. The pair dug up the treasure beside a large rock, after utilizing an occult ritual to avert the pirate curse, including a "preparatory ceremony, such as drawing a circle round the rock, and reciting some words of incantation." They dug with their spades until they discovered, to their excitement, an ironclad chest. Their elation rapidly became horror, however, when they looked up into the sky to see the apparition of a headless man swooping down upon them. The men quickly dropped their shovels and fled in terror, looking back only once to see the spot "enveloped in smoke and blue flame." Regaining their courage the next day, they returned to the island only to discover that their spades had disappeared, the ground had smoothed over, and no trace remained of the treasure.[3]

This incident, though fragmentary and undated, nevertheless remains the best documented supernatural legend of the island. Much less supportable is the third and last curse. Like that of William Kidd, this curse also involves buried treasure.

This particular legend begins in Mexico in 1721. Legend says that five sailors discovered the lost treasure of Guatmozin, a Mexican emperor, in a cave somewhere in Mexico and brought it back to Milford, Connecticut. Four of the five met "terrible deaths," whether at the hands of each other or the colonial authorities is unclear. The fifth sailor then hid the treasure in the basement of the old Milford Inn, where it was soon after discovered by a drunk searching the basement for beer. Before word could reach the colonial authorities, the sailor took the treasure upon his rowboat in the dead of night and rowed it to Charles Island. There, he buried the booty in secret. What later became of this sailor is unknown, only that he never returned to claim his stolen prize. The curse in this tale seems not to come from the sailor, but from the stolen Mexican gold of Guatmozin, which apparently brings a terrible doom anyone who touches it.

The triple curse of Charles Island is said to manifest in two ways; financial doom and ruin to anyone who builds on the island, and death by drowning for those who attempt to swim the channel separating it from the mainland (traversing the sandbar by foot is relatively safe, providing it is done at low tide). If one considers these incidents as valid indications of a curse, then the evidence becomes overwhelming. A brief recitation of several examples should illustrate the point.

As previously noted, farming enterprises on the island since the seventeenth century all met with failure. This trend continued well into the nineteenth century. During the War of 1812, three British vessels anchored at Charles Island briefly. This incident occurred on 1 October 1814. Though Milford militiamen posed no real threat to the warships, the British fled in a hurry, shortly after midnight. This has caused some to speculate that something they witnessed on the island had frightened them off.

In 1835, Major John Harris of New York City purchased the island for $800. He built an elaborate mansion on the highest ground, spending an additional $14,000 landscaping the region to resemble a peaceful English countryside. No sooner had this landscaping been completed when Harris's health took a serious downturn. He was forced to sell off the property in 1841, after which the island again changed hands in rapid succession for a number of years, until its purchase by Elizur E. Prichard for $2,500 in April of 1852.

Prichard had big plans. Recently retired, he had made for himself a substantial fortune as a button manufacturer. He invested an additional $10,000 to landscape the area for an elaborate and exclusive resort. Prichard opened his Charles Island House hotel to the public in June of 1853. He lived in the mansion with his wife Betsey and three daughters, Elizabeth, Katherine, and Sarah. Things looked promising in the beginning. The place became a popular retreat for sea captains, wealthy gentlemen, and their ladies, who gave the place considerable business.

Then Prichard's daughter Elizabeth died, just a year after the resort opened. Then, in late summer of 1859, a mysterious fire destroyed the barn adjacent to the hotel. Also destroyed in the fire was a prize horse and harness. The horse had been successfully pulled from the burning barn but then, inexplicably, broke loose of its handler and charged back into the flames and a fiery doom. Prichard himself was injured by over exertion trying to put out the flames. He was taken away, bleeding internally, and treated by Dr. Beardsley of Milford.[4]

Prichard's days on the island were numbered, however. Be it a lingering illness, an incomplete recovery from the fire, or the ancient curse, he lost his life while trying to leave the island on Thanksgiving Day, 1860. While walking the sandbar toward the mainland, he suddenly cried out for help and collapsed. The water was rising at the time. He was dragged to shore by two hunters who heard his cry, only to die in their arms. He was fifty-five years old.

Ownership of the island fell to his daughter, aspiring author Sarah Prichard, along with considerable debt from his failed enterprise. Sarah leased the island to a group of investors who restored the resort, which thrived again for a time. These constructive improvements served only to briefly stave off the inevitable, however. The experiment failed to generate the necessary income to remain in business, closing its doors in 1868.

The island was next leased from Sarah Prichard by the Miles Company, a fertilizer and fish oil manufacturer. A factory was soon built on the island and began processing between eight and fifteen million fish a year into menhaden oil. It seemed to thrive for the next decade, until the company went belly up, and Milford folk decided that they had had enough of the fish oil stink that drifted into their town. A court order from the town and financial litigation caused the Menhaden Fisher to close down in 1886.

Sarah nearly convinced the prestigious American Yacht Club to lease and restore the old hotel in 1884 but then, just when things looked promising, disaster struck again. A mysterious fire again erupted, on 1 August 1884, burning the entire resort to the ground. Without the buildings, the Yacht Club deal fell through, leaving Sarah and her financial partners heavily in debt.

Foreclosure came in 1888, followed by the purchase of the island by another New Yorker, Elizabeth F. Noble, who in turn sold it to the Connecticut Railway and Lighting Company. The CR&L originally planned to build an amusement park on the island, but plans fell through. The company became absentee owners and the island lay neglected for a dozen years.

Charles Island's next occupants remain, perhaps, the best known even though they remained for a mere decade. The circumstances of their arrival, activities, and mysterious departure have caused no small amount of speculation among the curse proponents.

In September of 1927, Father Edmund A. Baxter, a Dominican priest of St. Mary's Roman Catholic Church in New Haven, announced plans for his order to purchase Charles Island for the creation of a religious retreat. Shortly afterward, the CR&L Company sold the property and construction began on a retreat for priests and laymen.[5]

If any group of individuals could break the triple curse of Charles Island, these Roman Catholic priests were sure to do so. At least, that's what the locals figured. The curse, however, seems to have proved stronger even than the piety of these holy men. It was not long before tragedy struck.

Father Baxter certainly was not one to be deterred by any legends of a curse. A true soldier of God, he had served as an Army chaplain in World War I and, as such, was no stranger to adversity. A charismatic organizer, he assembled volunteer teams of laymen and teenagers to construct the parish, chapel, recreation hall, and several cabins. Walking paths through scenic woodland soon connected several simple stone shrines, dubbed the Stations of the Cross. Estimated construction costs of the St. Aquinas Retreat were about $100,000, with facilities to accommodate up to fifty men.

On 30 March 1929, even before the retreat officially opened, a dreadful calamity occurred. Six volunteer workmen from New Haven, including five men and a teenage boy, attempted to row back to the mainland after a day of work at the retreat. One of the men, John Balmer, served as caretaker at the retreat and was a resident of the island. Somehow, the boat capsized only a 1,000 yards from the island and all six drowned in the icy waters. The other drowning victims were fifteen-year-old high school student Walter Fallon, former Fire Commissioner William H. McDonald, his son, Burton V. McDonald (a plumber), laborer Sabato Del Franco, and carpenter John Clerkin.[6]

The bodies of Clerkin and Balmer were not recovered. To Father Baxter fell the onerous task of breaking the news to Balmer's wife, who lived on the island. The Balmers' son, Russell, was at the time in a seminary in Ohio, preparing to enter the priesthood.[7]

A stone shrine of St. Christopher was built on the island, as a memorial to the six dead volunteers. The facility's opening, only a few months later, was a somber one. Several shrines with statues of saints were erected, along with a stone bell tower with pointed Gothic arch. For several years, the chapel (accommodating sixty-five persons), dining hall, private ferry, power plant, and twenty-three cabins served Catholic clergymen and lay persons seeking spiritual succor. The place was praised for its natural beauty, simple woodland paths, and shrines.

By September of 1936, however, the Dominicans had decided to abandon the retreat, without explanation. The island and all twenty-five buildings were offered for sale by Father Dow, as representative of St. Mary's Church. Most telling of all, is a short sentence in the *Hartford Courant* article that covered the abandonment of the island by its holy men; "The Dominicans have made no plans for future retreats nor have they chosen any property as a successor to the island development."[8]

Had Curse triumphed over Church? Subsequent events argue that perhaps it had.

New Haven County High Sheriff Slavin proposed to purchase the property and its buildings from the Dominicans, in order to establish a First Offenders Crime Prevention Club. The sheriff hoped to use the sanctuary as a camp for juvenile offenders, as the natural beauty of a woodland retreat seemed infinitely preferable to internment in an urban lockup. It was not to be, however.

Just as it seemed the sale would go through, the great Hurricane of '38 hit. In the aftermath, it was discovered that almost all traces of the St. Aquinas Retreat had been obliterated by the storm's fury. Every building, every shrine, even the stone bell tower were gone. Only the remnants of a few foundations remained.

Perhaps it was a last-ditch effort that prompted thirty-five Roman Catholic priests to revisit and assess the island in late August of 1939. In light of everything that had occurred, perhaps they should have known better.

Embarking on the island's forty-foot cruiser, they found themselves caught in a sudden and violent storm. Soon shipwrecked upon the shore of Charles Island, they found no shelter remained for them, nor food, nor any immediate rescue. They endured two miserable days and nights waiting for the storm to abate and rescue to come. Finally, authorities commandeered two power boats from the Milford Yacht Club and retrieved the thirty-five priests, escorting them safely to shore. If there had been any doubt remaining in their minds about abandoning Charles Island for good, this incident certainly banished them.[9]

If Charles Island is truly cursed, then this curse certainly extends to the deadly channel separating it from the mainland. These seemingly placid waters have claimed more lives than anyone can seem to count. Some were claimed by the icy depths when their boat capsized, others waited too long to cross the sandbar and foolishly attempted the crossing after the water had begun to rise. Some valiant few attempted to rescue others in distress, making the ultimate sacrifice themselves for their efforts. The following is a list, by no means comprehensive, of many who have drowned in this channel.

July 1923, seventeen-year-old John J. Finn drowns, despite the rescue efforts of his two companions, after stepping into "two deep holes" off Charles Island. His body is not be recovered until several hours later.[10]

July 1928, a canoe with five occupants capsizes near Charles Island. Twenty-year-old Bessie Wollschlager of Meriden decides to make the swim to shore, while her fiancé, Chester Closson saves two younger girls and another man, Joseph Strong, saves himself. Bessie, though a good swimmer, is claimed by the undertow and drowned.[11]

April 1929, six New Haven volunteers working at the St. Aquinas Retreat drown when their boat capsizes on the return journey.

July 1939, five boys walking on the sandbar connecting Charles Island to the mainland, despite rising water, are hit by a pair of waves larger than the rest. Three of the boys are thrown into the water by the waves, though one is successfully rescued by the two oldest. Forrest Kwaack, age eleven, and Anthony Pagano, age seven, are pulled in by the undertow and drowned.[12]

August 1957, Gilbert Koplowski, age nineteen, drowns while swimming near Charles Island. He had been swimming back from the island with three teenage companions, when he got an attack of cramps and slipped below the surface. His body is located three hours later by a sixteen-year-old diver, in forty feet of water.[13]

May 1967, Pietro Persio, age fifty-one, drowns when his boat capsizes near Charles Island. His body is later found by police floating in the Sound.[14]

July 1972, Ralph Wells, age twenty-one, is skin diving with three companions when the current sweeps him away. His body is recovered days later, only fifty feet from Charles Island.[15]

Charles Island now belongs to the Department of Environmental Protection. Though open to the public, the interior is fenced off and closed from 1 May through 31 August, to protect rookeries of herons and egrets. These protected birds are now the island's only occupants, which is probably for the best since permanent residence on the island by humans seems decidedly unhealthy.

Although open to the public during the rest of the year, prospective hunters of pirate treasure will be frustrated to learn that no digging of any kind is allowed on the island. The sandbar from Milford's Silver Sands Park can be crossed safely at low tide, but be sure to time the return trip before the water rises. As you can see from the list above, curse or no curse, the current is deadly!

And if you happen to see the ghost of an Indian chieftain, pirate captain, or Mexican emperor... best to steer clear!

Chapter 12
Captain Grant Miracles

Captain Grant's Inn of Poquetanuck, may still be the home of the spirits of Mercy Adelaide Grant and her children. Note the double front doors, a renovation of spinster sisters who owned the inn and could not bear each other's company.

Not every haunting is malevolent, or even unwelcome. In fact, many believe that every region of intense negative energy has a nearby counterpart, a place of spiritual healing that counterbalances the negative. If this theory is true, then few better examples can be found than Captain Grant's Inn off Route 2A, in the sleepy little Connecticut town of Poquetanuck.

Located only a mile and a half from the infamous old Norwich Asylum (see Chapter 10), which housed the very worst of Connecticut's criminally insane from 1904 until 1971 and believed to be haunted by tormented spirits of former inmates, Captain Grant's Inn offers welcome and restful lodging in a historic little building, not far from Mystic and the Ledyard casino. Its popularity is due to more than just location, charm, and its rich history, however. The inn has its own style of haunting, its spirits are reputed to have the power to heal, both spiritually and physically, select living souls.

Located at 109 Route 2A, nestled in quiet, rural Poquetanuck across the street from the local cemetery, Captain Grant's Inn is owned and managed by a charming couple, Ted and Carol Matsumoto. Much of the previously unpublished ghost legends recounted here were gleaned through personal conversation between Carol Matsumoto and me.

Mrs. Matsumoto hesitated at first when recounting the most amazing parts of the story, those of the beneficial aspects of Captain Grant's invisible residents.

"Most ghost hunters don't want to hear this part," she would say with a friendly smile, as we sat on the inn's deck that warm September day in 2007. "I guess it's not spooky enough."

Headstones of William and Nathan Whipple, the original patriarchs of Captain Grant's Inn, from an overgrown and forgotten private colonial cemetery behind the inn.

The village of Poquetanuck dates back to 1687, though settlers probably existed there earlier. The field behind Captain Grant's Inn used to be a meeting place where Mohegans traded with Dutch and English and would later serve as a colonial burial ground. Archaeological digs have been done in this field and several interesting artifacts recovered.

The building is on the National Register of Historic Places. Built by a Mr. Whipple in 1754, it would later be inherited by his female descendant, Mercy Adelaide Avery. The Whipples are buried in the overgrown graveyard behind the inn, their headstones still visible today. Mercy Adelaide married Captain William Gonzales Grant, a sea captain who made further additions to the home. Captain Grant died at sea near Cape Hateras in 1810, at the age of thirty-two, leaving his pregnant wife and two children. He had been

Headstone of Mercy Adelaide Grant in Poquetanuck's cemetery. Does Adelaide still haunt her old homestead?

a notorious poker player, regularly taking to sea when he found himself in debt. On his last fateful voyage, he had been saddled with a green crew. While attempting to fix the ship's rigging, he got tangled and fell to his death on the deck. He had one boot on, and one still stuck up in the rigging.

The youngest son, also named William, was born in May of 1811, and would grow up to be a sea captain like his father. Mercy Adelaide lived to a ripe old age in the house, dying at the age of eighty-five. Captain Grant, his wife Mercy Adelaide, their son, William, and his wife, Sarah, are all buried across the street in the Poquetanuck Cemetery. The Adelaide Room at the inn is named in the memory of Mercy Adelaide, whom many believe still visits the room and knocks upon its door at odd hours.

During the Revolutionary War, American soldiers were billeted in the attic. Runaway slaves were also housed in the attic during the Civil War. Either of these two events may explain the footsteps and noises that guests still hear coming from the otherwise empty attic during their stays.

Sometime in the early 1900s, the Taylor sisters inherited the home. A pair of spinsters who hated each other's company, had had renovations made to the place that effectively cut it in half, so that neither would have to endure the other's company. There are two front doors for this reason, and the wide staircase leading to the second floor was originally partitioned in halves by a wall. The Taylor sisters lived into their eighties, and are also buried across the street in Poquetanuck Cemetery.

The home was then bought at auction in 1954 by James and Betty Congdon, who lived in the home with their three children and grandchildren until Betty died of bone cancer in the 1980s. Betty is also buried across the street. James left immediately afterward, renting the home for the next six years to the Barry family.

Carol bought the home on 13 February 1994. She and her husband, Ted Matsumoto, an engineer, have since lovingly restored the grand old colonial home to its former glory. Never having lived in the home itself, they rent its rooms overnight to tourists and vacationers. It is from these boarders that many of the personal accounts of unexplained phenomena have been gleaned.

Carol has witnessed a few of these events herself. Most common, she says, is a loud rapping at the front door. She has answered the mysterious knocking only to find nobody standing outside, across the street, or in the holly bushes flanking the door. One time that this occurred, at 10:00 pm on Christmas of 1985, Carol brought her camera and photographed a misty apparition outside the door (this photo she will kindly show anyone who asks respectfully). She has seen glowing orbs surrounding the painting of a ship in the common area, and discovered objects, particularly cleaning supplies, to have disappeared from one room of the inn only to reappear in another. This translocation of objects seems to be a fairly common event at the inn.

Also common are phantom footsteps, knocking upon doors, and objects moving of their own accord, as reported to her by boarders. The most active places in the home for these phenomena are the attic and the Adelaide Room.

Captain Grant's Inn, the Adelaide Room, where the apparition of a girl child has been seen, voices heard, and footsteps from the empty attic above.

Bathroom of the purportedly haunted Adelaide Room at Captain Grant's Inn, where the shower curtain rod moves and topples of its own accord.

In the bathroom of the Adelaide Room, the shower curtain rod has been known to fly violently out of its brackets. Six years ago, according to Carol, it jumped off and struck a maid in the head. When examined, the rod was found to be ten inches shorter than previously. This sort of phenomena continued, ultimately requiring the Matsumotos to replace the rod three times, gluing it in place, then screwing it into the wall. None of this seems to have prevented the rod from flying out and falling down at odd times, however.

Amy, a maid who had worked at Captain Grant's for the Matsumotos, was an atheist. She had also been suffering from a rare and potentially terminal condition that required experimental brain surgery. Some time prior to leaving for Boston General to have this surgery, she had been cleaning the bathroom of the Adelaide Room, when an event occurred which shocked her out of her previous skepticism. She later told Carol that she had been leaning down to clean the floor or tub, when the apparition of a girl child in antiquated clothes suddenly walked out of the wall and through her hands. The experience had not frightened her, however, instead a feeling of peace and well being overwhelmed her. Shortly afterward, Amy underwent the three-hour surgery in Boston and recovered immediately. She was ever afterward convinced that the ghostly girl had something to do with her miraculous recovery.

Carol also recalls an interesting pair of boarders, a couple who had run upon hard times. The couple had formerly been a priest and nun, who fell in love and abandoned their religious calling to be together. They had difficulty adapting to a more secular life, poverty and tragedy and the loss of their faith drove them into a downward spiral that led to drug addiction, specifically morphine. They spent a night in the Adelaide Room and woke to find themselves overcome with a feeling of peace and spiritual well being that they had not felt in many years. They left Captain Grant's the next day... without their morphine, having no further need of it.

A New York City police detective who spent a night in the Adelaide Room complained the next morning to Carol of a restless night, due to someone tramping about with booted feet in the attic between the hour of 4:00 am and 5:00 am. He was shocked to hear that nobody had been in the attic all night, and that the attic had housed Revolutionary War soldiers more than 200 years ago.

Victoria, a seventy-year-old woman with two daughters, spent a night in the Collette Room. She had spent the night alone, but said that she had felt someone's hand brush her check while she lay in bed.

Reports such as these have appeared in various newspapers and television media, quoted on Captain Grant's website. Indeed, the 31 October 2003 issue of *USA Today* included Captain Grant's in its national list of "10 Best Places to get in bed with a ghost."

The article states, "Be prepared for strange knocks at your door at unexpected hours... Guests who stay in the Adelaide Room are likely to have contact with the mysterious woman and her two children who once lived at the inn, built in 1754." A simultaneous 2003 broadcast on CNN Headline News cited Captain Grant's as being "one of the best places to stay if you would like to encounter a ghost."[1]

"The home is peaceful," says Carol Matsumoto. "Our guests say that it exudes warmth and love. Many wonderful things have happened here. I call them the 'Captain Grant Miracles.'"

Seaside Connecticut's Other Haunted Inns

Captain Grant's is not the only inn with a reputation for haunted happenings. Visit the historic Red Brook Inn at Mystic, also on the National Register of Historic Places, for more history and unexplained happenings. Also, New London's Lighthouse Inn, where people have seen a White

Mystic's Red Brook Inn, listed on the National Register of Historic Places, also believed to be haunted.

Monte Cristo Cottage on Pequot Avenue, New London. Only a short walk from the Lighthouse Inn, and believed to be haunted by the mother of American playwright Eugene O'Neill.

Lady on the staircase, believed to be a bride who fell down the stairs and broke her neck on her wedding day. While in New London, a short walk or drive from the Lighthouse Inn will bring you to the historic Monte Cristo Cottage on Pequot Avenue, former home of American playwright Eugene O'Neill, also believed to be haunted.[2]

New London's Lighthouse Inn, believed to be one of Connecticut's most haunted.

Chapter 13

Remington's Restless Shades

Remington Arms Factory in Bridgeport, site of several disasters
and deaths, and believed to be haunted by shadowy apparitions.

Sitting neglected and abandoned in downtown
Bridgeport, in the trouble-plagued neighborhood
of Helen Street and Barnum Avenue, are the
remains of what was once one of the world's largest arms
and munitions factories. Remington Arms supplied much
of the ammunition and firearms for our troops and allies
throughout both World Wars, though a casual observer
would not guess by viewing them that the three remaining
rectangular brick buildings, vacant and decayed, were
once part of a sprawling 120-acre industrial community
employing up to 17,000 workers in its heyday. Much of the
original complex has been sold and developed over, only a
portion of which remains today. For over a century, people
lived, worked, and sometimes died on the grounds.

The Remington Arms plant's worst disaster occurred in 1942, during the height of World War II, when an explosion occurred in the ammunition packaging building, killing seven workers and injuring more than eighty. The building was destroyed, nearby box cars overturned or demolished, shards of glass, bullets, and flames were sent flying into nearby factory buildings and homes. People whose homes were suddenly rocked by the explosion and whose windows and doors were suddenly riddled with bullets, dove for cover, fearing a German raid. Newspapers reported the possibility of sabotage by conspiring Nazi sympathizers, and a lengthy investigation by the FBI, Military Intelligence, Connecticut State Police, and other government agencies followed, the reports of which were never made public.

Today, the eerie skeletal buildings have a reputation for being haunted by shadowy entities that flit past the empty windows and gaping holes in the decrepit brick walls. Eyewitness accounts of these shadow apparitions, whom some speculate to be the restless shades of Remington's

past, can easily be found online via the Shadowlands website and others. Adventurous urban explorers have returned from the ruins and underground tunnels with their own photographs and stories, though a professional paranormal investigation presents difficulties. The location lies within a high-crime neighborhood, the buildings are structurally unsafe for exploration, and legal wrangling over the place has left the fate of the property and its historic buildings in doubt.

Our story of the Bridgeport Remington factory's glorious and tragic past begins on 6 August 1867, with the incorporation of the Union Metallic Cartridge Company (UMC), specializing in production of the newly invented metallic cartridges. Business thrived so much that, in 1912, the industrial giant Remington Arms Company purchased the small factory and combined to become Remington UMC. In the years leading up to World War I, production grew at an enormous rate until the factory complex dwarfed nearly all of the world's arms factories. Though it continued to make sporting guns, military rifles and ammunition quickly became its primary export to England and France, as well as filling the growing U.S. military contracts as American involvement in the Great War became inevitable. The project was hailed for its contribution to the war effort, as well as the huge economic boom it brought to Bridgeport.

Yet even from the beginning, and throughout its glory days, the Remington plant in Bridgeport had its own dark history of violence and tragedy...

The plant was growing rapidly in July of 1915, when a workers' strike turned violent. The riot seems to have begun with a dispute between disgruntled Portuguese workers and guards at the plant. Guards armed with wooden batons responded to a call for help from one of their fellow guards, whom workmen were about to throw in an eight-foot ditch. A melee ensued and police were summoned to the scene as a full-fledged riot broke out, eventually involving a hundred workers, twenty guards, and the Bridgeport Police. One newspaper described the scene, "men were lying here and there where they had fallen." Frank Monte, an eighteen-year-old worker, had to be rushed to St. Vincent's Hospital with a fractured skull from a guard's baton.[1]

By July of the following year, twelve million dollars (an enormous sum in 1916!) had been spent in developing the huge factory complex. In a little over eight months, the property had grown amazingly from the single UMC factory building to thirty-eight separate buildings encompassing every stage of arms and munitions manufacturing, packaging, and shipping. Guards recruited from prior army and navy men, 800 strong and organized as a military company, patrolled the grounds. While even the largest arms factories in war-torn Europe were pumping out six or seven thousand rifles a day, the Remington plant routinely turned out 10,000 a day.[2]

As with any factory that manufactures explosives, accidental explosions happened. The first, in May of 1929, had no fatalities. Two powder magazines burst, causing thousands of dollars in damage, but only one injury. The plant had fortunately been closed to observe the Memorial Day holiday, thus staffing at the plant was minimal.[3]

In fact, the first documented death at the plant had nothing to do with explosives. John O'Shea, a seventeen-year-old workman, was electrocuted and died while cleaning a motor in July of 1934. He accidentally touched a 230-volt wire.[4]

In the years leading up to World War II, the Remington company collaborated with the U.S. government in the creation of several more ammunition plants. As war loomed, production, as well as profits, again sped up for the company. Enemy sabotage was always a concern as the Bridgeport factory expected to be another major contributor to the war effort, as it had in World War I.

Ironically, two years before the horrific 1942 explosion, an anonymous caller had given a tip to authorities that the Remington Arms plant in Bridgeport would be sabotaged, with catastrophic results. The mysterious tipster, described as "husky-voiced," placed the call to a police precinct in Brooklyn, New York. Though the factory head scoffed, local police took the call seriously enough to cordon off the area and search the entire grounds for nine hours before assigning a special police guard at the site. The caller simply stated that the factory "would be blown up during the day."[5]

On Saturday, 29 March 1942, just before 2:00 pm, at the little packing building in the northwest corner of the sprawling Remington Arms plant (at what was then the intersection of Helen Street and Berkshire Avenue), a sudden explosion occurred that rocked the city for miles in every direction. The bodies and lives of seven workers instantly hurled into oblivion, only fragments of which would ever be recovered. Another eighty were injured as flying bullets and shards of glass from shattered windows

Remington Arms Factory in Bridgeport, view of the shot tower, where molten lead was dropped to produce bullets.

ripped through nearby buildings. Many thought that the city had come under attack by German bombers. Among those killed were Miss Katherine Butler, fifty-two, of Bridgeport, Mrs. Ellen Hansen Potts, thirty-nine, of Bridgeport, Mrs. Ethel Gunther, twenty-nine, of Stratford, Mrs. Gertrude Stegeman, of Bridgeport, Ernest Bendetto, thirty-two, of Bridgeport, George Carrick, thirty-six, of Milford, and George Dutcher, forty-four, of Stratford. Many others suffered a variety of puncture wounds, lacerations, and burns.[6]

Fire, police, and medical professionals rushed to the scene as flames leapt to nearby homes and buildings. Many in nearby buildings were thrown from their feet in the force of the explosion as bullets whizzed through windows, walls, and doors over their heads. At a nearby loading platform, three box cars had been parked. One was reduced to scrap, utterly destroyed, the other two catapulted from their rails.[7]

The 3,600 square-foot building had been one of the smaller structures of the, by then, 550-acre complex. Two stories tall and built of red brick, it marked the end of the assembly line, where ammunition was packaged in wooden crates for shipment.[8]

After the initial chaos and disaster, work began again at the plant with only a very short delay. By the next morning, debris has been cleared and Remington announced that the plant was back in full production. The war effort was all important and any further delay was considered unacceptable. The company announced formally that they did not believe sabotage to be responsible for the disaster, that a nail driven into a packing crate had accidentally impacted a cartridge primer, causing the explosion. This announcement, however, did not prevent a full investigation by civilian, military, police, and government authorities.[9]

Indeed, a conspiracy of Nazi saboteurs was not ruled out. FBI agents took over investigations, with the aid of Fire Chief Martin Hayden, state Fire Marshal Lieutenant Eugene Lenzl, and State Police Sergeant William Visokay. Captain Donald Emerson MacKenzie, of military intelligence headquarters in Boston, also became involved, as well as air raid warden Frank T. Rohm.[10]

Despite Remington's assurances that no sabotage had happened, concern among various agencies proved significant enough to launch a private investigation by Coroner Theodore E. Steiber, who began interviewing witnesses separately from the plant authorities.[11] Even as late as April, the FBI admitted to reporters that their investigation into the explosion was far from complete.[12]

As ridiculous as a Nazi conspiracy in Connecticut may seem to us today, it seemed a very real possibility in the 1940s. The findings of these exhaustive investigations were never officially released (at least none that I was able to find), which makes one wonder about just what sort of data was uncovered. Unfortunately, the victims of the 1942 explosion were not the last to die at the Remington Arms plant.

In a much smaller explosion at the primer mixing building in 1978, Dominick Pulley, an employee of the plant for thirty-eight years and witness to the 1942 explosion, was killed while mixing chemicals for primer. No structural damage to the building and no other fatalities resulted.[13]

The post-war years saw a significant shrinking of the Bridgeport plant as property was sold off and developed for separate projects. In late 1988, the Remington company announced that it would be closing down its Bridgeport plant and moving its headquarters to Wilmington, Delaware. At that time, only 125 workers were still employed at the plant, primarily engaged in the manufacture of .22 caliber rimfire ammunition.[14]

After a failed experiment manufacturing and marketing Remington electric shavers, the company decided to abandon the Bridgeport property altogether. In 1986, it sold the property to RemGrit Realty, Inc. Use of the buildings was leased to several local businesses, known as "International Enterprise Park," by RemGrit until the company delivered eviction notices to them in 2005 to make way for extensive renovation and larger projects. This appears to have been the decision of local developer Salvatore DiNardo, who purchased a controlling interest in the firm. Complicating the issue of the historic buildings' future is a foreclosure action in Bridgeport Superior Court, in which $10 million in back taxes is allegedly owed.[15]

A November 2005 fire at the building fronting Barnum Avenue, believed to be arson, further damaged the already decrepit structure. Firefighters identified homeless persons living within the structure as having been the cause of the fire.[16]

Westport Capital Partners purchased the property in 2006 and is considering utilizing the site for a high-speed ferry, pending further information from the Bridgeport Port Authority.[17]

The future of the remaining Remington Arms buildings, with their distinctive red brick shot tower and a century of history, appears to be as mysterious as their past. What will become of them... and of the shades of Remington's past that lurk within?

Chapter 14
Milford's Unquiet Past

The Bryan-Downs House

Bryan-Downs House, property of Milford Historical Society on Wharf Lane, Milford. Our investigative group had interesting personal experiences while investigating this historic colonial home, where MHS members have experienced unexplained phenomena.

The eighteenth century Bryan-Downs House is one of three historic buildings currently owned by the Milford Historical Society, all located at 34 High Street. It has been remodeled over the years, restored, dismantled, moved, and reassembled upon its present location. Built around 1785 upon the old Post Road between Milford and New Haven by a Captain Jehiel Bryan, it has been occupied by at least three generations of his descendants. Originally a six-room saltbox-style home, its first occupants were Captain Bryan and his son, Jehiel Bryan, Jr.

The junior Jehiel Bryan had married one Mary Treat in 1784, and soon occupied the house with their daughter, Mary Esther Bryan. This daughter later wed Ebenezer Downs of Waterbury, with whom she continued to live in the same house. Their son, Ebenezer Downs, Jr. inherited the house in 1837, and wed Miss Esther B. Camp in 1848.[1] He enlarged and remodeled the home, removing the original stone chimney and fireplaces, and erected a smaller chimney. He also rebuilt the front hall and stairs to the second floor, and made the covered walkway to the barn into a summer kitchen.

Upon the death of Ebenezer Downs, Jr., the family turned the house into a rental property. It was dismantled, moved to the Milford Historical Society property and rebuilt in 1977. It still retains much of the original siding and the front windows.

On the first floor, south side, is displayed the Claude C. Coffin Indian Collection. Many interesting Native American artifacts can be found here. Also on the first floor is a gift store and meeting room. On the second floor is a small reference library. Not much else is currently known about the history of the home's inhabitants.

Our interest in the Bryan-Downs House was actually secondary. I had contacted the Milford Historical Society to request permission to investigate the Eells-Stow House. It was only after we had gained permission to investigate all three historic homes that we were told of reported paranormal activity that had been occurring in the Bryan-Downs House. One of the most interesting reports came from Ellen, a member of the MHS. She had been cleaning upstairs on the second floor, alone in the house, when she heard her name being called. She had also been touched by an entity or entities on at least two occasions. Other members have felt they were watched while alone in the house.

Though the Bryan-Downs House did not seem to have any documented incidents of trauma, tragedy, or unusual historic events that might indicate a likelihood of paranormal activity, it seemed that eyewitness accounts pointed to the contrary.

We therefore, of the three historic homes available, decided to investigate the Bryan-Downs first.

Our Investigation

We arrived at the historic Bryan-Downs House on the evening of Saturday 13 January 2007. We had a full team, including myself, Matt, Gail, Seth, Haydon, Trisha, Trica, and our newest investigator-in-training, Cynthia. Also present were Rosanne, as representative for the MHS, Autumn Pinette, a photojournalist for the *Connecticut Post*, and David Springer, a television reporter for Channel 12. David Springer had made prior arrangements with the MHS and us to be imbedded in the investigation. Though we had done interviews for television and newspapers before investigations, this was our first time having imbedded media within the investigation. Though we appreciated the positive publicity such a thing would generate, evidence contamination was also a concern. Fortunately for us, the media persons were very friendly and made every effort to follow our protocols.

Seth and Matt set up infrared video cameras throughout the house, while Haydon and Cynthia set up audio recording equipment. The rest of us made ourselves busy unloading equipment, loading fresh batteries and taking our turns at being interviewed by Channel 12. Teams of two were organized and assigned separate tasks, such as getting base EMF and temperature readings throughout the house, positioning voice recorders, and taking digital photographs.

We then turned out the lights and retired to the basement, where we had set up our headquarters, for a couple hours to let the equipment record without human interference. Then Gail was ready to do her walk-through and Sensitive communications. I accompanied her with my EVR (electronic voice recorder) and digital camera. Trisha followed with a Nightshot-enabled Sony handycam. Autumn, of the Post, followed and photographed while David, of Channel 12, filmed with his own Nightshot Sony handycam.

Gail sensed the first entity after we walked out of the annex and into the living area, just before the gift store. She felt the presence of a young woman whose name she believed to be Marjorie. Marjorie, she said, had been a supervisor among the domestic staff, in her early twenties. Though Gail considers herself more of a clairaudient and clairsentient than clairvoyant, she felt that Marjorie had generally worn a cap and long skirt while going about her sundry duties. Marjorie's spirit felt perpetually rushed and frantic, like she had been saddled with more responsibilities than her experience had prepared her for. She was always tidying, supervising, preparing for guests or whatever events the master of the house had planned. She was not a distressed entity, or even a powerful one, more of what I generally refer to as a "spirit echo" of someone who had once been firmly attached to the place.

The second presence Gail sensed in the same location. This was the master of the house, whose name she suspected was Paul. She described him as a middle-aged, well-dressed and mustached man, whose short temper and powerful demeanor had been a little frightening to his domestic staff in life. He had an aristocratic bearing and wore a watch fob. Gail felt he had known Marjorie in life, but had no strong or personal attachment to her. Like Marjorie, he seemed to be merely a spirit echo, not necessarily aware of our presence in the house at all. He seemed consumed with his own duties, a busy and important business man.

In the Indian Artifacts room, Gail sensed many strong attachments to the artifacts. She felt they were unhappy about their tools and artifacts being put on display. No specific individual personalities presented themselves, only a general feeling of subdued or latent hostility. It was in this room that both Trisha and Tricia had inexplicable camera malfunctions that had not seemed to affect anyone else's equipment.

From downstairs, Gail felt a much more powerful presence pulling her upstairs. She went up the staircase, through a storage area and directly into the research/reference room where Ellen of the MHS had felt a presence touch her and her name being called. Gail said the room had once been the bedroom of a "Lady of the House," who would not give her name. This entity, Gail felt, was the most powerful in the house. Gail felt she had been a frail and frantic woman, who suffered from some illness, either real or imagined. The Lady had lost at least one child (possibly two miscarriages) and had never again tried for more, nor recovered from the loss physically or psychologically.

The Lady had delegated many of the tasks that would normally have been hers, as mistress of the house, to domestic staff such as Marjorie. The Lady was a distressed spirit, but not one that would allow Gail to help her. She was aware of our presence, but too consumed with her own unhappiness to really care. Gail felt the Lady typically wore a "frothy" nightgown, or bedclothes.

I asked Gail if the Lady had ever made herself known to anyone living (thinking of Ellen's experience, of which Gail was unaware). Gail then told us that she had. The Lady had made her presence known to another woman, whose voice she had found comforting since it reminded her of an aunt or grandmother she had known in her early life. I asked Gail if the Lady could describe the living woman she had made herself known to, and how the Lady had tried to communicate. Gail said the Lady had done little things, like trying to blow in the living woman's ear, and had done so to an older woman with graying hair, a soft-spoken voice, and eyeglasses (this was an accurate description of Ellen). Gail felt that the Lady was a petulant spirit who enjoyed attention, and was often in her bed. No physical bed remained in the room, only file cabinets, books, and reference materials. This would prove to be the most interesting part of the night.

Haydon later tried a question and answer session with the Lady, Gail, and Cynthia, in hopes of capturing EVPs. Unfortunately, no EVPs were gleaned.

We wrapped up the on-site investigation and interviews in the early morning hours and left, after saying our thanks and goodbyes to Rosanne. Over the next several weeks, we reviewed many hours of video footage, voice recordings, and countless photographs from several different cameras. Unfortunately, no hard data presented itself. Some video anomalies we had to discount as dust orbs. Also, we realized too late that much of our early voice recordings were hopelessly contaminated from too much foot traffic and too many people speaking.

In the days following the on-site investigation, Dirk Perrefort of the *Connecticut Post* interviewed me via telephone for an article that afterward appeared in the paper. A separate article by MHS member and reporter Frank Juliano also appeared in the *Post*. The online version of the articles contained many of Autumn's color photographs of the house and our team, taken during the investigation. NBC 30 interviewed MHS President Susan Carroll-Dwyer about the investigation, the segment airing on the 6:00 pm news. Publicity from the event generated more requests for residential investigations from private homeowners, as well as historic investigations by nearby Historical Societies.

Even though we were disappointed that we had no hard data to present the MHS, we were grateful to them for allowing us the opportunity to investigate such a worthy site. They had granted us permission to investigate all three of their buildings, and we could not wait to do the others.

The Eells-Stow House

The Eells-Stow House, home of the Milford Historical Society on Milford's Wharf Lane site. Site of Captain Stow's heroic effort to save 40 Revolutionary soldiers infected with smallpox, an effort which cost him his own life. One very good EVP was gleaned from this investigation by our team.

Built sometime between 1670 and 1680 by Milford colonist Samuel Eells, and the only property of the Milford Historical Society that remains on the same spot where it was originally built, this colonial home is unique for its architectural qualities as well as its history. Experts of colonial architecture will tell you about its old purlin and ridge scheme roof, the projected cornice, the original lean-to, and the unique dog-legged stairs.[2]

Most interesting to historians, however, is the home's later owner, Captain Stephen Stow. His heroic effort to save the lives of smallpox-infected American soldiers in his own home, ultimately cost him his life. A large granite obelisk in nearby Milford Cemetery, marking the mass grave of forty-six of the doomed soldiers and Captain Stow, tells his story best.[3]

Captain Stow Monument, Milford Cemetery, marks the mass grave of Captain Stow and the Revolutionary War soldiers he tried to save, all of those buried here died of smallpox.

One side of the Soldiers' Monument, 1777, reads:

"IN HONOR OF FORTY SIX AMERICAN SOLDIERS WHO SACRIFICED THEIR LIVES IN STRUGGLING FOR THE INDEPENDENCE OF THEIR COUNTRY; THIS MONUMENT WAS ERECTED IN 1852, BY THE JOINT LIBERALITY OF THE GENERAL ASSEMBLY; THE PEOPLE OF MILFORD AND OTHER CONTRIBUTING FRIENDS. TWO HUNDRED AMERICAN SOLDIERS, IN A DESTITUTE, SICKLY, AND DYING CONDITION WERE BROUGHT FROM A BRITISH PRISON SHIP, THEN LYING NEAR NEW YORK, AND SUDDENLY CAST UPON OUR SHORE, FROM A BRITISH CARTEL SHIP, ON THE FIRST OF JANUARY, 1777. THE INHABITANTS OF MILFORD MADE THE MOST CHARITABLE EFFORTS FOR THE RELIEF OF THESE SUFFERING STRANGERS; YET, NOTWITHSTANDING ALL THEIR KIND MINISTRATIONS, IN ONE MONTH, THESE FORTY SIX DIED, AND WERE BURIED IN ONE COMMON GRAVE. THEIR NAMES AND THEIR RESIDENCES ARE INSCRIBED ON THIS MONUMENT. WHO SHALL SAY THAT REPUBLICS ARE UNGRATEFUL?"

Conditions for captured American soldiers were indeed horrific. Smallpox outbreaks were common, as were other diseases, starvation, death, and abuse by British captors. It was not uncommon for the British to unload their unwanted, diseased human cargo at American ports and afterward fire the ship. Says one historian, describing the conditions aboard the British prison ship, *Whitby*, "No medical men attended the sick, disease reigned unrelieved, and hundreds died of pestilence or worse, starved, on board this floating prison."[4]

On another side of the obelisk, Captain Stow's sad tale is told:

"IN MEMORY OF CAPT. STEPHEN STOW OF MILFORD, WHO DIED FEB. 8, 1777, AGED 51 YEARS. To administer to the wants and soothe the miseries of these sick and dying soldiers, was a work of extreme self denial and danger, as many of them were suffering from loathsome and contagious maladies. Stephen Stow voluntarily left his family to relieve these suffering men, he contracted disease from them, died, and was buried with them. He had already given four sons to serve in the War for Independence. To commemorate his self-sacrificing devotion to his country, and to humanity, the Legislature of Connecticut resolved that his name should be inscribed upon this monument."

The British prison ship unloaded its 200 diseased prisoners of war upon Milford harbor on New Year's Day, 1777. The shocked town folk rushed to their aid, despite their dreaded fear of the disease. Stephen Stow, Milford's town doctor at the time, brought many of them into his own home. Some of the worst off died that first day. The following day, the soldiers were relocated to a town hospital, where Stow continued to treat them. Before he left, he put his affairs in order and made out a legal will to provide for his family. He had already lost four sons in the war.

He would soon afterward contract the disease himself, sicken, and die in his own home. Forty six of the 200 soldiers also died, and were buried with him in a mass grave at Milford Cemetery. The death toll probably would have been much higher had it not been for the heroic efforts of Captain Stow in treating the sick even when his own health waned. Though he may never have raised a musket, Captain Stephen Stow is certainly one of our country's most courageous wartime heroes.

Our Investigation

I was fully aware of Captain Stow's story long before our team investigated the nearby Bryan-Downs House of Milford. In fact, the Eells-Stow House was my primary reason for contacting the Milford Historical Society in the first place. If death, suffering, and great events could leave behind energies that become genuine hauntings, then I figured the Stow House to be a great place to test this theory.

Witnesses of actual phenomena in the place were few. Two of the MHS members said they had felt like they were being watched when alone in the place. The two present caretakers of the home, though they believe in the paranormal and have stayed in other historic homes they believed to be haunted, described the Stow House as the "least haunted" place they had stayed in. Previous caretakers, however, I was told had witnessed unexplainable events.

By the time we got around to investigating the Stow House, we had already investigated both the Bryan-Downs and the Stockade House. Lack of any hard data gleaned from either of these investigations was discouraging. We had captured not a single anomaly in our photographs or video, and not one EVP on our recorders to share with the generous folks of the MHS. We had some interesting personal experiences, true, but these things are easily scoffed at by skeptics and nearly impossible to substantiate. In our investigation of the Stockade House, in May of 2007, both Matt and Haydon

Stockade House, another of the three properties owned and operated by the Milford Historical Society, where two members of our investigative team heard what sounded to be a baby crying.

heard what sounded to be a baby crying in the house, but none of the audio equipment picked it up.

We investigated the Eells-Stow House on a warm August night in 2007. Rosanne was with us again, as MHS representative, and investigators included Matt, myself, Haydon, Trisha, and Jenn. We had with us some new infrared equipment we were eager to try out and Haydon brought a new audio recording setup that NASA would have been proud of. This new audio recording equipment of Haydon's would turn out to serve us very well, and capture our only hard paranormal evidence of the night (also one of our best EVPs yet!).

Our investigation was typical of others we have done. Video and audio were setup, photos taken, EMF and temperature readings gathered. Jenn felt a profound sadness from the large painting downstairs (actually a copy of a rare seventeenth century portrait of Samuel Eells) and from the children's room upstairs. Toward the end of the night, we all gathered in a circle in the kitchen to do a Question and

Standing in front of the Bryan-Downs House in Milford, from left to right, Channel 12 reporter David Springer who accompanied us as a imbedded media on our investigation, myself, MHS President Susan Carroll-Dwyer, and Ellen the MHS member who experienced unexplained phenomena in the historic home.

Answer session for EVPs. It was then that we captured what we have since labeled a Class "A" EVP.

During the session, Matt asked the question, "Do you not want us here?"

Later review of the audio would show that three seconds after he finished the question, he was answered. All of us who listened agree that the voice says "Get Out!"

This is a fairly common EVP, but is remarkable for its clarity and that it was recorded at only 183 Hertz. It stands up to rigorous analysis. The fact that it seems to answer Matt's question may also indicate an intelligent haunting. We were happy to finally have some hard evidence to share with the Milford Historical Society. We left the Stow House, hoping to return at some future date.

Conclusion

Like much of seaside New England, Connecticut's shore is steeped in legend and mystery. It's coast looks out upon Long Island Sound, better known to the original colonists as "The Devil's Belt," whose dangerous reefs and narrow channels have earned its points of access names like "Hell's Gate." As the mist rising off the Sound envelops these shorefront properties on foggy nights, so these legends and traditions of ghostly happenings envelope sleepy Connecticut towns, infusing the communities with a peculiar pride in their own local ghosts and spirits.

These tales have been handed down from generation to generation, as oral traditions or footnotes in local histories. Witches, pirates, ghosts and curses populate these tales, each with a seed of truth reaching back into nearly four centuries of Connecticut's past. Who's to say which tales are real and which ones not?

Keep this in mind if you find yourself walking the mist-shrouded Connecticut shore at night, with only the distant, eerie foghorn for company as cold tendrils crawl up your spine and into your very bones. No need to turn around... those footsteps you hear behind you are merely echoes of your own... or are they?

Endnotes

Ghost Ship of New Haven

[1]John Warner Barber, *Connecticut Historical Collections* (Hanover, New Hampshire: University Press of New England, 1999), 161.

For Whom the Bell Tolls

[1]"Loss of the Atlantic, Further Particulars," *Hartford Daily Courant* (reprinted from the *Norwich Courier*), December 1, 1846, page 2.

[2]"The Atlantic, The Coroner's Inquest," *Hartford Daily Courant* (reprinted from the *Norwich Courier*), December 4, 1846, page 2.

[3]"Awful Calamity!" *Hartford Daily Courant* (reprinted from the *Norwich Evening Courier*), November 30, 1846, page 2.

[4]"Loss of the Steamer Atlantic and Many Lives," *Hartford Daily Courant*, November 30, 1846, page 2.

[5]"The Wreck of the Atlantic," *Hartford Daily Courant* (reprinted from the *Boston Atlas*), December 12, 1846, page 3.

[6]"The Ill Fated Atlantic and Her Noble Commander," *Hartford Daily Courant*, December 11, 1846, page 2.

[7]"Loss of the Steamer Mohegan," *Hartford Daily Courant*, December 29, 1846, page 2.

[8]David Philips, *Legendary Connecticut* (Willimantic, Connecticut: Curbstone Press, 1992), 204 thru 207.

[9]Harlan Hamilton, *Lights & Legends, A Historical Guide to Lighthouses of Long Island Sound, Fishers Island Sound and Block Island Sound* (Stamford, Connecticut: Wescott Cove Publishing Company, 1987), 198 thru 207.

Nightmare On Elm Street

[1]Troy Taylor, *The Haunting of America* (Alton, Illinois: Whitechapel Productions Press, 2001), 19 thru 29.

[2]William Wilcoxson, *History of Stratford* (Bridgeport, Connecticut: Brewer Bors Corp., 1939), 711.

[3]"The Stratford Mysteries," *Hartford Daily Courant* (reprinted from the *New Haven Palladium*), April 27, 1850, page 2.

[4]"The Stratford Rapping," *Hartford Daily Courant* (reprinted from the *New Haven Journal*), May 1, 1850, page 2.

[5]Reverend Dr. Eliakim Phelps, "The Stratford Mysteries and Knockings in General," *Hartford Daily Courant* (reprinted from the *New York Observer*), July 4, 1850, page 2.

[6]Rufus Jarman, "Mystery House on Elm Street," in *Mysterious New England*, ed. Austin N. Stevens (United States: Rodale Press, Inc., 1979), 136 thru 147.

[7]Owen, Dana, "In Stratford, an ice cream shop with lots of spirit," *Connecticut Post*, June 29, 2006.

[8]"Stratford on the Sound," *Lippincott's Magazine*, July, 1897, page 33.

Midnight Mary

[1]David Philips, *Legendary Connecticut* (Willimantic, Connecticut: Curbstone Press, 1992), 232 thru 236.

[2]"Mrs. Hirth Woke Up, Not a Minute Too Soon, Though," *The Hartford Courant* (reprinted from the *Chicago Times Herald*), January 22, 1900, page 7.

[3]Harold Castner, "Was She Buried Alive?" in *Mysterious New England*, ed. Austin N. Stevens (United States: Rodale Press, Inc., 1979), 296 thru 301.

[4] "Two Jail Breakers Caught in New Haven," *The Hartford Courant*, July 11, 1933, page 12.

[5]Richard M. Kaukas, "Missing Girl's Clothing Found Near Cemetery," *The Hartford Courant*, September 25, 1970, page 6.

[6]"Attempted Suicide on Her Daughter's Grave," *The Hartford Courant*, November 1, 1897, page 11.

[7]"Couple at Cemetery Mistaken For Ghosts," *The Hartford Courant*, December 18, 1939, page 4.

[8]"Calls From Her Grave? Excited Hungarians Say Minnie Bedner Was Buried Alive," *The Hartford Courant*, August 17, 1905, page 1.

The Essex Rappings

[1]"Mysterious Rappings In Essex House Accompany Spirit Messages By Girl," *The Hartford Courant*, January 24, 1915, page 1.

[2]"Ghost's Ghost Still Lingers in Essex," *The Hartford Courant*, January 31, 1915, page 3.

[3]"Essex 'Spirit' Exposed By Two Women, Girl In Bed Made the Raps, Boy Helped," *The Hartford Courant*, January 25, 1915, page 1.

[4]"Essex Girl Who Lost a Ghost," *The Hartford Courant*, January 30, 1915, page 1.

[5]"Essex Spirits Fail To Save Brown Home," *The Hartford Courant*, February 11, 1915, page 1.

[6]"May Vanderbilt Discusses Essex Ghost Rappings," *The Hartford Courant*, February 8, 1915, page 1.

The Bridgeport Poltergeist

[1]Paul F. Eno, *Faces at the Window* (Woonsocket, Rhode Island: New River Press, 1998), 15.

[2]Laurence Cohen, "'Ghost's' Clatter Rattles Family," *The Hartford Courant*, November 26, 1974, page 1.

[3]Laurence Cohen, "Girl Admits Bedeviling Home," *The Hartford Courant*, November 27, 1974, page 6.

[4]Ed and Lorraine Warren, *Ghost Hunters* (New York, New York: St. Martin's Paperbacks, 1989), 210.

The Lighthouse Keepers

[1]Jeremy D'Entremont, *The Lighthouses of Connecticut* (Beverly, Massachusetts: Commonwealth Editions), 135 thru 143.

[2]Michael Golay, "Lighthouse Faces a New Era as Technology Replaces Crew," *The Hartford Courant*, April 1, 1984, page B1.

[3]George Steitz, *Haunted Lighthouses and How to Find Them* (Sarasota, Florida: Pineapple Press).

[4]Beth Pollard, "Era Passes for Lighthouses As Automation Takes Over," *The Hartford Courant*, October 15, 1978, page 41A4.

[5]Roger Catlin, "Fleshing Out the Ghosts," *The Hartford Courant*, June 7, 2005, Life Section.

[6]Roger Catlin, "'Ghost Hunters' In New London," *The Hartford Courant*, August 31, 2005, Life Section.

[7]William Thomson, *Lighthouse Legends & Hauntings* (Kennebunk, Maine: 'Scapes ME), 88.

[8]"Keeper of Penfield Reef Light Drowns in Gale," *The Hartford Courant*, December 26, 1916, page 1.

[9]Jeremy D'Entremont, *The Lighthouses of Connecticut* (Beverly, Massachusetts: Commonwealth Editions), 37 thru 47.

[10]Harlan Hamilton, *Lights & Legends; A Historical Guide to Lighthouses of Long Island Sound, Fishers Island Sound and Block Island Sound* (Stamford, Connecticut: Wescott Cove Publishing, Co.), 77, 78.

[11]"Bridgeport Yacht Explodes, Sinks At Penfield Reef," *The Hartford Courant*, June 7, 1953, page B11.

[12]"Youths Rescued by Coast Guard," *The Hartford Courant*, May 17, 1966, page 28E.

Secret Deaths at Seaside

[1]"Cass Gilbert Will Design Sanatorium," *The Hartford Courant*, August 13, 1923, page 1.

[2]"Buildings Ready at Seaside for Sanatorium Use," The

Hartford Courant, December 23, 1934, page B1.

[3]"Seaside Center Mismanagement Charged," *The Hartford Courant*, March 14, 1972, page 39D.

[4]David H. Rhinelander, "Seaside Center Hearings Open," *The Hartford Courant*, July 11, 1972, page 10.

[5]David H. Rhinelander, "More Abuse Charges Voiced In Retarded Center Hearing," *The Hartford Courant*, July 18, 1972, page 6.

[6]David H. Rhinelander, "Expert Praises Finn, Seaside Center at Hearing," *The Hartford Courant*, August 10, 1972, page 11.

[7]Carolyn Battista, "Changes to Help Retarded," *The New York Times*, September 8, 1985.

[8]Elizabeth Hamilton and Dave Altimari, "Fatal Errors, Secret Deaths," *The Hartford Courant*, December 2, 2001, page A1.

Elizabeth Hamilton and Dave Altimari, "How Did They Die? The State Won't Say," *The Hartford Courant*, December 3, 2001, page A1.

[9]Tom Condon, "Adrift At Seaside," *The Hartford Courant*, May 21, 2006, page C4.

Haunted Battlefield

[1]Alfred Cave, *The Pequot War* (Amherst, Massachusetts: University of Massachusetts Press), 151.

[2]Charles Alley, ed., *The Battle of Groton Heights: A Collection of Narratives, Official Reports, Records, etc.* (New London, Connecticut: Higginson Book Company, reprint), various narratives.

[3]John Warner Barber, *Connecticut Historical Collections* (Hanover, New Hampshire: University Press of New England, 1999), 310.

[4]Betsey Barber Larrabee, *The Story of the Battle of Fort Griswold and Groton Heights Monument* (Groton, Connecticut: DAR, 1960), 4.

Norwich Insane Asylum

[1]Corey Sipe, "History of Norwich State Hospital," *Associated Press*, November 2, 2006.

[2]"Norwich Asylum Opened," *The Hartford Courant*, December 9, 1904, page 2.

[3]"Lawyer E.K. Arvine Hangs Himself in Asylum," *The Hartford Courant*, December 1, 1914, page 1.

[4]"Explosion Kills Man at Insane Hospital," *The Hartford Courant*, March 16, 1919, page 18.

[5]"State Hospital Cook Dies of Injuries," *The Hartford Courant*, April 18, 1925, page 3.

[6]"Nurse, Insane Patient, Kills Self With Knife," *The Hartford Courant*, April 4, 1930, page 12.

[7]"Insane Man Kills Norwich Police Sergt.," *The Hartford Courant*, December 12, 1934, page 1.

[8]"State Probes Man's Death at Norwich," *The Hartford Courant*, December 3, 1941, page 5.

[9]"Kills Wife With Bread Knife; Had Been in Asylum," *The Hartford Courant*, September 30, 1918, page 1.

[10]"Boy Murderer Declared Insane," *The Hartford Courant*, January 21, 1922, page 15.

[11]"Admits Choking Baby, Mother Becomes Insane," *The Hartford Courant*, March 21, 1928, page 4.

[12]"John Palm Held Insane, Life Saved," *The Hartford Courant*, February 25, 1938, page 1.

[13]"Mother Held in Child's Death Declared Insane," *The Hartford Courant*, August 19, 1938, page 18.

[14]"Action Taken on Hospital by Governor," *The Hartford Courant*, September 19, 1944, page 1.

[15]"Parents' Slayer Ordered Kept in State Hospital," *The Hartford Courant*, May 23, 1952, page 2.

[16]"The 'Cain and Abel' Case," *The Hartford Courant*, January 31, 1954, page SM3.

[17]"Dynamite Killer Transferred to State Hospital," *The Hartford Courant*, August 12, 1954, page 3.

[18]"Murder Trial Planned for Cooley, Found Sane," *The*

Hartford Courant, July 3, 1957, page 6B.

[19]"Slayer of Two Children Cleared, Sent to Hospital," *The Hartford Courant*, March 23, 1961, page 1.

[20]"Stabbing Suspect to Stay in Hospital," *The Hartford Courant*, September 22, 1972, page 10.

[21]Patricia Barnes, "Accused Slayer Called Insane," *The Hartford Courant*, June 8, 1974, page 8.

[22]Robert Murphy, "Mental Patient Slaying Suspect," *The Hartford Courant*, May 22, 1976, page 1.

[23]Lisa Richardson, "A father's killing 16 years ago still haunts his family; Tragedy's pain still fresh after 16 years," *The Hartford Courant*, March 8, 1992, page A1.

[24]Joseph Cohen, "Man Pleads Guilty in Slaying; Judges Find Him Incompetent," *The Hartford Courant*, December 18, 1982, page B5B.

[25]Lynne Garnett, "Man Found Responsible in Mother's Slaying," *The Hartford Courant*, October 16, 1984, page B2.

[26]"Point Raised That Hopelessly Insane Be Put To Death," *The Hartford Courant*, February 6, 1921, page 1.

[27]"The Norwich Investigation," *The Hartford Courant*, June 16, 1939, page 14.

[28]"The People's Forum: Norwich Hospital," *The Hartford Courant*, May 16, 1946, page 8.

[29]Gerald Demeusy, "State Police Probe Hospital Violence," *The Hartford Courant*, April 25, 1967, page 1.

[30]Edmund Mahony, "Hospital Workers Protest Assaults, Staff Size," *The Hartford Courant*, August 6, 1982, page B6A.

[31]David Rhinelander, "Norwich Closing Security Center," *The Hartford Courant*, September 15, 1971, page 1.

[32]David Rhinelander, "Infamous Unit to Close," *The Hartford Courant*, September 19, 1971, page 3B.

[33]Amy Lawson, "VH1 films 'Paranormal Project' at Norwich State Hospital," *Norwich Bulletin*, June 21, 2006.

Thrice Cursed Island

[1] John Warner Barber, *Connecticut Historical Collections* (Hanover, New Hampshire: University Press of New England, 1999), 229 thru 238.

[2] Kathleen Schuman, "This island's for the birds," *Milford Mirror*, April 11, 2001.

[3] Michael Dooling, *An Historical Account of Charles Island* (Milford, Connecticut: The Carrollton Press, 2006), ent.

[4] "Fire on Charles Island," *Hartford Daily Courant* (reprinted from the *New Haven Palladium*), August 2, 1859, page 2.

[5] "Dominicans Buy Island For Retreat," *The Hartford Courant*, September 25, 1927, page A1.

[6] "6 Drown As Boat Upsets Off Milford," *The Hartford Courant*, March 31, 1929, page 1.

[7] "Bodies of Four Drowning Victims Found in Sound," *The Hartford Courant*, April 1, 1929, page 1.

[8] "Charles Island and Its Buildings Offered For Sale By Dominicans," *The Hartford Courant*, September 30, 1936, page 13.

[9] "35 Priests Rescued From Charles Island," *The Hartford Courant*, September 1, 1939, page 2.

[10] "Youth, 17, Drowned Off Charles Island," *The Hartford Courant*, July 17, 1923, page 18

[11] "3 Persons Drown In Connecticut," *The Hartford Courant*, July 9, 1928, page 1.

[12] "New Britain Boy Saves Another But Two Others Drown In Milford," *The Hartford Courant*, August 1, 1939, page 1.

[13] "Shelton Youth Drowns Despite Rescue Effort," *The Hartford Courant*, August 14, 1957, page 10A.

[14] "Boat Capsizes, Man Drowns," *The Hartford Courant*, May 14, 1967, page 4B.

[15] "Body of Man, 21, From Milford Found in Sound," *The Hartford Courant*, July 20, 1972, page 8.

Captain Grant Miracles

[1]"10 great places to get in bed with a ghost," *USA Today*, October 31, 2003.

[2]Dolores Riccio and Joan Bingham, *Haunted Houses USA* (New York, New York: Pocket Books, 1989), 263 thru 266.

Remington's Restless Shades

[1]"Strike Riots at the Remington Arms Factory," *Lost Angeles Times*, July 15, 1915, page 11.

[2]"Our Greatest Arms Plant," *The Washington Post*, July 5, 1916, page A19.

[3]"Powder Magazines Blow Up at Bridgeport; Remington Plant Blast Rocks Wide Area," *The New York Times*, May 31, 1929.

[4]"Boy, 17, Electrocuted In Bridgeport Factory," *The Hartford Courant*, July 22, 1934, page C6.

[5]"Remington Plant Plot Is Doubted," *The Hartford Courant*, September 18, 1940, page 2.

[6]"Bridgeport Blast Deaths Placed at 7," *The Hartford Courant*, March 30, 1942, page 1.

[7]"Blast Bodies Recovered," *New York Times*, March 31, 1942, page 19.

[8]Milton Bracker, "3 Dead, 6 Missing In Munition Blasts," *New York Times*, March 29, 1942, page 1.

[9]"Death Toll Mounts In Munition Blasts," *New York Times*, March 30, 1942, page 19.

[10]"Six Probably Dead, 80 Injured In Bridgeport Munitions Blast," *The Hartford Courant*, March 29, 1942, page 1.

[11]"Private Probe of Blast In Bridgeport Planned," *The Hartford Courant*, April 9, 1942, page 3.

[12]"Remington to Replace Blast-Wrecked Building," *The Hartford Courant*, April 5, 1942, page A5.

[13]"Man Killed In Blast at Arms Plant," *The Hartford Courant*, December 14, 1978, page 77.

[14]James Ayres, "Remington Plant Closing," *The Boston Globe*, December 18, 1988, page 94.

[15]Susan Silvers, "Artisans stunned by eviction," *Connecticut Post*, August 11, 2005.

[16]Bill Cummings, "Remington factory burns," *Connecticut Post*, November 4, 2005.

[17]Rob Varnon, "Housing planned for Remington site," *Connecticut Post*, June 21, 2006.

Milford's Unquiet Past

[1]"Marriages." *The Hartford Courant*, January 15, 1848, p.2

[2]Norman Isham and Albert Brown, *Early Connecticut Houses* (New York, New York: Dover Publications, Inc., 1965), 138.

[3]H.F. Randolph Mason, *Historic Houses of Connecticut Open to the Public* (Essex, Connecticut: The Pequot Press, 1969), 8.

[4]Louis F. Middlebrook, *Maritime Connecticut During the American Revolution* (Salem, Massachusetts: The Essex Institute, 1925), 170.

Bibliography

Allyn, Charles, ed., *The Battle of Groton Heights: A Collection of Narratives, Official Records, etc. of the Storming of Ft. Griswold.* Salem, Massachusetts: Higginson Book Company, 1882.

Barber, John W., *Connecticut Historical Collections.* Hanover, New Hampshire: University Press of New England, 1999.

Bingham, Joan and Riccio, Dolores, *Haunted Houses USA.* New York, New York: Pocket Books, 1989.

Cave, Alfred A., *The Pequot War.* Amherst, Massachusetts: University of Massachusetts Press, 1996.

Citro, Joseph A., *Passing Strange, True Tales of New England Hauntings and Horrors.* Boston, Massachusetts: Houghton Mifflin Company, 1996.

Cross, Wilbur L., comp., *Connecticut: A Guide to Its Roads, Lore, and People.* Cambridge, Massachusetts: The Riverside Press, 1938.

D'Entremont, Jeremy, *The Lighthouses of Connecticut.* Beverly, Massachusetts: Commonwealth Editions, 2005.

Dooling, Michael C., *An Historical Account of Charles Island.* Milford, Connecticut: The Carrollton Press, 2006.

Dudley, Gary P., *The Legend of Dudleytown: Solving Legends through Genealogical and Historical Research.* Bowie, Maryland: Heritage Books, Inc., 2001.

Eno, Paul F., *Faces at the Window.* Woonsocket, Rhode Island: New River Press, 1998.

Godbeer, Richard, *Escaping Salem, The Other Witch Hunt of 1692.* New York, New York: Oxford University Press, 2005.

Grant, Ellsworth S., *Connecticut Disasters: True Stories of Tragedy and Survival.* Guilford, Connecticut: Morris Book Publishing, LLC, 2006.

Hall, David D., *Witch Hunting in Seventeenth Century New England*. Boston, Massachusetts: Northeastern University Press, 1999.

Hamilton, Harlan, *Lights & Legends: A Historical Guide to Lighthouses*. Stamford, Connecticut: Wescott Cove Publishing Co., 1987.

Heermance, Edgar L, comp., *The Connecticut Guide: What to See and Where to Find It*. Hartford, Connecticut: Emergency Relief Commission, 1935.

Isham, Norman M. and Brown, Albert, *Early Connecticut Houses*. New York, New York: Dover Publications, Inc., 1990.

Larrabee, Betsey B., *The Story of the Battle of Fort Griswold and Groton Heights Monument*. Groton, Connecticut: Anna Warner Bailey Chapter, Daughters of the American Revolution, 1960.

Mason, H.F. Randolph, *Historic Houses of Connecticut Open to the Public*. Essex, Connecticut: Pequot Press, 1966.

Middlebrook, Louis F., *Maritime Connecticut During the American Revolution*. Salem, Massachusetts: The Essex Institute, 1925.

Orr, Charles, ed., *History of the Pequot War: The Contemporary Accounts of Mason, Underhill, Vincent, and Gardiner*. Cleveland, Ohio, 1897.

Perley, Sidney, *Historic Storms of New England*. Beverly, Massachusetts: Commonwealth Editions, 1891.

Philips, David E., *Legendary Connecticut*. Willimantic, Connecticut: Curbstone Press, 1992.

Radune, Richard A., *Pequot Plantation: The Story of an Early Colonial Settlement*. Branford, Connecticut: Research in Time Publications, 2005.

Revai, Cheri., *Haunted Connecticut: Ghosts and Strange Phenomena of the Constitution State*. Mechanicsburg, Pennsylvania: Stackpole Books, 2006.

Ritchie, David and Deborah, *Connecticut: Off the Beaten Path*. Guilford, Connecticut: The Globe Pequot Press, 2002.

Robinson, Charles T., *True New England Mysteries, Ghosts, Crimes & Oddities*. North Attleborough, Massachuesetts: Covered Bridge Press, 1997.

Steitz, George C., *Haunted Lighthouses and How to Find Them*. Sarasota, Florida: Pineapple Press, 2002.

Stevens, Austin N., ed., *Mysterious New England*. United States of America: Rodale Press, Inc., 1993.

Taylor, John M., *The Witchcraft Delusion in Colonial Connecticut*. Bowie, Maryland: Heritage Books, Inc., 1989.

Taylor, Troy, *The Haunting of America*. Alton, Illinois: Whitechapel Productions Press, 2001.

Tedone, David., *A History of Connecticut's Coast*. Hartford, Connecticut: Coastal Area Management, 1982.

Tomlinson, R.G., *Witchcraft Trials of Connecticut*. Hartford, Connecticut: The Bond Press, Inc., 1978.

Thomson, William O., *Lighthouse Legends & Hauntings*. Kennebunk, Maine: 'Scapes ME, 1998.

Trumbull, Benjamin, *A Complete History of Connecticut, Civil and Ecclesiastical: From The Emigration Of Its First Planters, From England, In The Year 1630 To The Year 1764 And To The Close Of The Indian Wars*. Kessinger Publishing (reprint of the 1818 edition).

Warren, Ed and Lorraine and Chase, Robert D., *Ghost Hunters*, New York, New York: St. Martin's Paperbacks, 1989.

Wilcoxson, William H., *History of Stratford*. Bridgeport, Connecticut: Brewer Bors Corp., 1939.